THE NATURE OF LOVING

PATTERNS OF HUMAN RELATIONSHIP

VERENA KAST

Translated by Boris Matthews

Chiron Publications • Wilmette, Illinois

Originally published in 1984 as *Paare*
Copyright 1984, Dieter Breitsohl AG

Translation © 1986 by Chiron Publications
Library of Congress Catalog Card Number: 86-17125

Edited by Deborah Farrell
Book design by Lauretta Akkeron
Printed in the United States of America

Library of Congress Cataloging-in-Publication Data

Kast, Verena, 1943–
    The nature of loving.

    Includes index.
    1. Love. 2. Interpersonal relations. I. Title.
BD436.K3313   1986   158'.24   86-17125
ISBN 0-933029-06-3

Second printing, 1990

Contents

Preface

In fantasies of relationship, which we nurture and savor especially in periods when we are intensely in love, we idealize our partner as well as those aspects of ourselves that our partner touches. This idealization corresponds to the essence of love. Through such fantasies the best in ourselves is liberated, and we can transcend what we have become. Fantasies of relationship underlie every relationship, even if we are not aware of such fantasies.

In my work with people in mourning, I continually find that acceptance of death is easier for those who are aware of the fantasies underlying their relationships. Such individuals understand which fantasies bound them to their partner when their relationship was most vital and which aspects of their own personality their partner enlivened. These people feel robbed by their partner's death, but they are also aware of what cannot be taken from them in their partner's death.

The crucial work in mourning is often the laying bare of the fantasies of relationship. These fantasies, which change in the course of a lifetime, can reveal the meaning of the relationship in terms of an individual's development and life.

Mythological images of the sacred marriage underlie these fantasies of relationship. The unions celebrated by Shiva and Shakti, Ishtar and Tammuz, Zeus and Hera, for example, depict the union of heaven and earth necessary to bring about the origin of all life and to sustain life's fertility. In discussing the myths of sacred marriage, I intend to show how human relationships, depicted in accounts, dreams, fantasies, and literature, mirror the relationships of such divine couples.

I hope to stimulate in the reader an awareness of the significance of fantasies within a relationship as well as intrapsychically. Such fantasies of relationship awaken archetypal feminine and masculine elements in a specific combination in each partner and create feelings of wholeness, vitality, and of creative ecstasy.

Chapter 1

ON THE FERRY TO THE OTHER SHORE

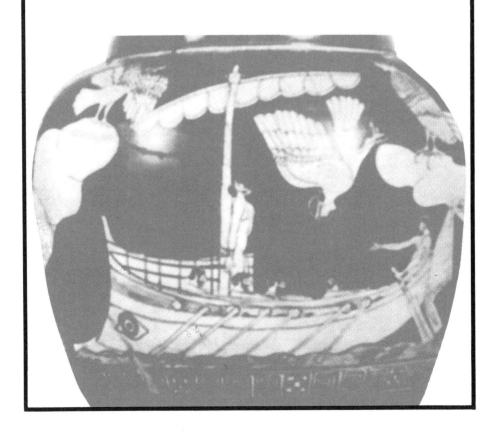

Since all life is love maturing,
And the life of life is spirit.
　　　　　　　　　　—Goethe

The sequence of images in the following dream conveys a fantasy of relationship:

> I left our mountainous landscape and set out walking along a river. I felt myself
> to be alone and also free, but the feeling of homelessness outweighed the feeling of freedom. I continually looked about myself to see whether or not I might
> catch sight of a familiar face. I knew no one. There were men there whom I
> feared because they looked so brutal, and the other people there all seemed turned in
> upon themselves and took no notice of me. Gradually it became clear to me
> that I was not threatened, except that no-one paid attention to me.
> Where a bridge used to lead across the river, there was, as in olden times, a
> woman who ran a ferry. There was a young man with her. They seemed to love each
> other very much, although it was not expressed in their gestures. It was simply
> obvious. He was young—also somehow old—and had the look of a young man
> who always has new ideas. She was wonderously beautiful, foreign, very careful, and
> completely absorbed in her work. Both of them, actually, were concentrating intensely
> on their work.
> I felt a terrible longing to belong to them, to be accepted by them. As long as I
> remained on the boat, I was in their realm; I felt their self-containment, their involvement with each other, and their common devotion to a task.

As he gradually awoke, he tried to prolong his awakening. A deep sadness
seized him because he sensed that those two would also be separated; they
would not be able to remain a unity: "And then I again succeeded in calling back the atmosphere of their oneness. . . . Those two did not have the
effect of humans, but of gods made human."

This is the dream of a twenty-eight-year-old man who had made the acquaintance the previous evening of a woman who fascinated him. He had spent
part of the night letting fantasies of a relationship with the woman take shape:
He imagined how he would meet her the next time and what he would say
to her; he saw himself with her in various situations; he conceived a conversation
between them; he invented pet names for her and also imagined what pet
names she would invent for him. . . . When he finally fell asleep, he had the dream
that deeply moved and preoccupied him. He was especially touched by the
divine yet human couple. Particularly fascinating to him were not the individual
figures, who were no longer clear to him on awakening, but rather their
ensemble. Their "unity," "oneness," and "common devotion to a task" were
words he used to describe the experience of the dream. In his associations he
repeatedly emphasized the word, *wholeness*: "I had the feeling of wholeness;
that's why I did not want to awake; that is, 'wholeness' and also 'mystery.'

This couple is a fascinating mystery to me: They may show me something entirely new in my life that could surpass anything I have yet experienced."

That he can experience something entirely new with the couple is already expressed in the image of the journey across the river to a new shore. Similarly, the emotional fascination the couple holds—which leads him to say that they seem to be gods made human—suggests a quality of transcendence.

The young man did not relate the couple in his dream to his fantasies of the previous night: The ferry woman did not seem to him to resemble the woman who had fascinated him so greatly the day before. He admired the wise young man in the dream who was not an excessively hardy sort but rather a meditative, clever man who seemed very much alive.

Since he had met this woman, he also felt very much alive, and just as the dream couple had concentrated on their task, he too wanted to concentrate on living the relationship. That was his ideal. He perceived the dream couple to be extraordinary, almost inhuman, whereas he described himself as completely ordinary; here again the couple in the dream represented one of his ideals.

Another aspect of the dream that preoccupied the young man was his leaving a familiar region, a place where he felt "at home." The awakening love is represented in the dream as his departing the land of his youth. In the dream he initially felt very alone, and his departure brought not only freedom but the loss of safety and security, as well as the anxiety of no longer being noticed in the new surroundings. The persons appearing in the dream represent aspects of the dreamer's personality; for example, the men who seemed brutal could be aspects of himself that are revealed in situations of uncertainty, signified in the dream by the departure. He fears that he could become brutal in a greatly exposed situation, but in the dream he did not stop at the frightening prospect. Instead, he followed the familiar river. When he came to the place on the river where one could usually cross, there was no longer a bridge. The river of his homeland had changed. Instead of the bridge there was a "ferry couple" who transported him to the other shore—to new possibilities.

This dream was probably triggered by his having fallen in love the previous afternoon and by his subsequent fantasies, which typify the condition of being in love. Fantasies during this time tend to be very lively and colorful, for a person in love is creative. We have fantasies not only when we are in love; we continually weave fantasies about our relationships.

It is typical that in fantasies of relationship, we not only fantasize an actual or a possible desired partner, but we also more or less consciously see ourselves as an idealized figure in these relationships. We imagine ourselves as we would like to be or could be for this beloved person. The dreamer did this when he admired the young man in his dream: He wanted to be meditative, clever, lively. By revealing that he feels so alive since he met this woman, he had indicated that through his fascination for the woman, a lively, clever, and wise side in him wants to come alive.

Every person who fascinates us taps something in our psyche that can then be brought to life. This creative potential is an extraordinarily important aspect of a relationship. What one person may draw from another cannot be lost, even when two people part. If those new aspects of ourselves that have been revealed in a relationship continue to be experienced and understood, we do not always lose ourselves when relationships dissolve. In love relationships these aspects are especially visible and accessible. Yet whatever becomes visible in an exceptional situation—and love is this—can also reveal itself in less dramatic relationships if our capacity for experiencing and our ways of perceiving have been sharpened.

The dreamer was not a clever person; he was a somewhat slow, circumspect man who lacked a certain flexibility. He was therefore very surprised that he was capable of creating such "daring" fantasies about himself and his possible partner.

In his fantasies of relationship as well as in his dream, the young man saw himself and the beloved in their idealized forms. But the kind of relationship he imagined also reflects the particular bent of both partners.

In the waking fantasies, the pet names are important to the dreamer. Pet names suggest a safe and protected relationship, and the names make each partner special. They also imply a very specific relationship that is rooted in a definite time. When at a later time a couple uses an earlier pet name, they both reach back to a fantasy that once formed the foundation of their relationship. Through the process of reaching back to earlier fantasies, they also immerse themselves in memories of experiences that bound them to each other at that time. Pet names thus convey change in a relationship and reveal facets that have significance only in connection with each partner.[1]

In the foreground of the dream was the unity of the couple, which was also revealed in their needing no gestures to depict their unity and in their devotion to their task. This state of unity is obviously the dreamer's relationship wish: He wants to approach a task with his partner devotedly and yet also cleverly.

If this dream couple is seen symbolically as a couple constellated in the soul of the dreamer and thus expressing possibilities of life for him, then they embody the possibility that he can live his life devotedly and with a feeling of wholeness, which is a feeling of happiness. But the dream couple also embodies the young man's fantasy of relationship: He would like to live with a woman as this couple lives. He later said that the couple represented an "ideal" for him. The dreamer is a person with many ideals and is rather skeptical when something looks so thoroughly ideal.

Fantasies of relationship involve the ideal. In such fantasies the beloved and the lover—as a part of the relationship to the beloved—are always idealized. Dostoevski captured the sense of this when he suggested that loving a person means seeing that person as God might have intended him or her. This statement can be broadened to mean that whenever we are loved, we also experience ourselves as God could have intended us. Such an experience is part of the essence of love. Perhaps love only arises and blossoms when we envision a beloved's best possibilities and are able to draw them out through love. These possibilities transport the beloved out of the narrowness of his or her life and open that person to something he or she had not thought possible. By eliciting a beloved's potential, the lover gains a part of that person, and something in the lover is also transformed in the process.

What we see in a beloved may be a "consolidated ideal,"[2] which needs the fantasy of a lover to incarnate it in everyday life. At first, however, only the lover's ideal may be involved. If that remains the case, disillusionment quickly follows. But a secret aspect of love is its power to grant us the vision and courage to see something in a partner which that person may have sensed but perhaps may never have known had it not been lovingly suggested by another.

In fantasies of relationship we project onto the beloved not only what we lack but what reaches out to us from our own psyche through another. The beloved is not only a mirror in which we can find ourselves; through love, we envision the best possibilities in the beloved and give that person the feeling that those possibilities can be realized. When we truly love, we will also forgive the beloved if those possibilities are not completely realized. The creative fantasies and feelings of anticipation involved in love bind us to the beloved, and we are capable of realizing our best possibilities as long as we maintain them in our fantasies.

This aspect of love is not to be understood as imaginative violence. Love and fantasy endow the lover with the ability to see in the beloved many possibilities that may not be seen by someone who does not love. What may seem to be the "blindness" of love is actually the gift of vision, the chance for love.

After the young man had fantasized a relationship with the woman, he had a dream that elevated his fantasies to the level of the ideal. The human but divine couple in his dream depict his ideal of a relationship. In all fantasies that have to do with everyday, loving interactions, something in them touches the "divine"; these fantasies have a transcendent quality, yet the ideals in such fantasies can be realized. Whenever we love, these ideal aspects of human existence are also touched, and qualities that we ascribe to the gods and that usually lie beyond our reach move into the realm of what can be lived, even if only in fantasy. Such ideals elevate a person's self-esteem and give him or her an immense push toward the realization of that person's most deeply concealed aspects. Even if such ideals can never be fully realized, they push an individual toward development and stand behind every love.

Fantasies involving ideals of relationship mirror the myths of the relationships between the gods. The traditional stories of relationships between gods frequently appear at some level in the fantasies of individuals. In such fantasies we are partly attempting to integrate the masculine and feminine aspects of our own psyche, and this process has a great influence on the way in which we relate to each other as men and women.

I would like to emphasize another important aspect of the young man's dream: the feeling of wholeness he experienced in relation to the ferry couple. This feeling of wholeness is an essential aspect of fantasies of relationship. A relationship idealized in fantasies, dreams, imagination, or in real life releases this feeling of wholeness in us; we are aware that we are undergoing a process of development and are in tune with life. We naturally seek a partner who can evoke this feeling of wholeness in us, for nothing can give us the sense of self-worth and well-being as can this experience of unity. Partners are not there, however, to maintain one's wholeness; they stimulate these images in us, draw them into life, and compel us to deal with these images and to incarnate them.

At the end of the dream, the dreamer did not want to awake and lose this feeling of unity. He perceived very clearly that not only the unity is a reality but also the separation, and on awaking he succeeded alternately in experiencing oneness and separation. Separation must be envisioned in every fantasy of relationship. People cannot live only in union; they are constantly forced to be individuals. Although the experience of separateness cannot be denied, it is still only one aspect of relatedness. In what follows it is necessary to discuss all aspects of relatedness: the ideals, the bonding behavior, and the inevitability of separation.

In summary, a fantasy of relationship always underlies our relationships with others. These fantasies are most compelling when we are in love; we are then seized by these fantasies—we give them form, we live in them.

My thesis is this: In a fantasy of relationship a couple is formed who partly reflect one person's ego but who also represent a stimulating, exciting union that promises happiness and wholeness, and all of this is set free by the partner. The fantasy reveals not only what the partner might be for the other person but also that person's idea of which characteristics the partner can bring to life in him or her. Such a fantasy embraces not only two individuals but also the relationship that these two have with each other, the joy and the satisfaction that arise, the fears that must be dealt with.

The images of the partners and the form of their relationship are dependent on many factors: the relationship of the partners to their parents; earlier relationships that have given them a sense of well-being; the social norms they have experienced (for example, in movies or on television). Archetypal images are also involved, as well as the yearning to feel wholeness in the experience of love and the need to find out again and again that separateness can become a transforming unity. In a fantasy of a relationship with another, however, the yearning for one's own wholeness lies hidden, as does the hope of overcoming the separateness from others.

A tremendously stimulating aspect of love is its ability to allow us through fantasies to see ourselves anew and to grow beyond ourselves. In love, each partner is seen as God could have intended him or her. There is a sobering side to love, of course: when we can no longer support these images and we begin to devalue each other, there is great disillusionment, and the promise of freedom through relationship becomes a threat of constriction and imprisonment.

Whether or not two persons enter a relationship probably depends on whether their fantasies of relationship correspond. In entering a relationship, we are attentive to whether or not our partner can realize aspects of our fantasy. We seek a partner who can enter our fantasies of relationship and enrich them; love occurs when the partner's fantasies correspond with our own.

If we are vital persons, we will find that these fantasies of relationship change again and again in the course of life, and thus we must continually share these fantasies with each other if we want to have strong relationships. Sharing the fantasies implies using them not as reproaches against each other but as yearnings for new, shared life. The fantasies then become the path markers of a common relationship. Crises and problems occur when we find that our partner cannot share (or is not yet capable of sharing) a new fantasy of relationship, or if we are not conscious of our new longings.

Myths as Models

The ideals submerged in and expressed through fantasies of relationship have varied relatively little in the course of time and among different cultures. Basic human longings and fears concerning relationship appear to remain the same; only our way of dealing with them changes.

The fundamental longings and fears connected with love and relationship have been depicted in the myths of divine couples handed down to us through the history of religions. Myths express how humans attempt to understand themselves and the world. The myths of divine couples are interpretations of the behavior of couples and are possible models for the relationship between men and women. Since there are various divine couples, there are also various models that are ideals with which we must come to terms.

Myths are the collectively valid stories of humanity concerning life and death; when we occupy ourselves with them, we continually discover levels of meaning through which our view of life may be explained or other perspectives may be revealed. If they no longer had any significance for our understanding of life and the world, we would no longer find them interesting. I believe that in attempting to explain phenomena such as fantasies of relationship, it is helpful to draw upon various interpretations of life so that a new way of seeing can be revealed from many perspectives.

If in fantasies of relationship, particularly in those associated with intense love, archetypal feminine and masculine energies are constellated in each person, with a simultaneous enlivening of the creative and the imaginative, then it must be possible to find such couples in mythology, literature, dreams, and the daily life of the individual. I will pursue this idea by presenting myths of divine couples; I will then show how these divine couples are embodied in literature or in contemporary people and how they affect fantasies of human relationships.

Chapter 2

SHIVA
AND
SHAKTI

The Ideal of Complete Union

We dreamt of one another
And from that we awoke,
We live to love each other,
And sink back into night.

You walked out of my dream,
From yours I stepped out, too,
We'll die if one of us
Gets lost in the other.

On a lily tremble
Two drops, pure and round,
Flow into one and roll
Down the calix's throat.
—Friedrich Hebbel

Image and Longing

Herbert, a thirty-five-year-old man, was successful in his middle-class profession but was less successful as an artist. After the first public showing of his work, he found he could no longer create anything new. He could justify why he was not active artistically, but he was immensely angry about his inactivity.

He was afraid that his second work might not be praised as much as his first and that people might be more demanding of him after his first success. He was also afraid that if he were to create again, he might lose himself so completely in his work that he would "flip out" or even become psychotic. (Many artists with a creative block use alcohol as an escape because they cannot sustain a great degree of overstimulation.)

Herbert formulated his ideal of relationship as follows:

I would like to have a partner who understands me completely, who shares my deepest thoughts, who has eyes only for me, as I have eyes only for her. I imagine that we would live in constant embrace, actually as well as symbolically, and that we would each be very creative. I would feel completely sure of myself, contained, understood, and strong, and she would, too. She would make my energies flow. But if she left me, my world would collapse; I couldn't bear that, and that's why now this fantasy is a longing that can never be fulfilled.

This man runs from every relationship as soon as it "sparks," that is, as soon as he has the feeling that something in him is tapped which he cannot control. He prefers calm, uncomplicated relationships that are based on clear agreements and that can be dissolved without major psychic exertion. Of course, these relationships could not stimulate him, either. There is a connection between his reluctance to resume the creative work that might overstimulate him and his reluctance to embrace a relationship in which his entire fantasy life would be freed. It is also obvious that his longing is to experience an entirely different form of relationship.

The images of this longing are images that appear in the creation myth of Shiva and Shakti. In this myth, love, relationship, and creation of the world are viewed as one. This oneness seems to me to be the essence of love, for in every love relationship a world arises for the two lovers, and love itself is very fertile. Procreation and birth, which are expressions of love, also symbolize the calling forth of something new in each partner that is tremendously enlivening and that enables each person to transcend past limitations. In the love relationship we see what is true for every relationship: Our essence always confronts us more clearly the more we involve ourselves openly with another person. Through a "thou" we become an "I." The ecstasy of creation characterizes love, and this is demonstrated clearly in the myth of Shiva and Shakti, which is both a creation myth and a love myth.

I will quote this creation myth extensively because it depicts essential aspects of ideals of relationship. My source is Heinrich Zimmer's *Adventures and Journeys of the Soul*.[1] Zimmer was the first person to translate the Shiva-Shakti myth into a European language.

Indian mythology regards Brahma, Vishnu, and Shiva as three aspects of the mother goddess, Maya; Maya is here understood as the "all-bearing womb, the all-nourishing breast, the all-devouring grave." Brahma is seen as the creator; he is responsible for the creative acts of the divine totality. Vishnu is the sustainer of the world who "guarantees its stability"; he is the savior and is responsible for rest. Shiva is called the "destroyer" but is also the "divine in motionless self-absorption: the eye turned inward, immersed in the ideal emptiness of his being" (p. 250). He does not participate in the fluctuations of life except in destruction, which in this myth is viewed as indispensable for the eternal flow of events.

The Origin of Relationship as Creation Myth

The text relates that Brahma brings forth the world with gods and other beings out of inner concentration. He sits in the circle of his "spirit-born" sons— the future seers and wisemen—and again sinks into "the contemplation of his innards" (p. 251).

Abruptly out of a new depth the most magnificent, dark haired woman appeared out of his visions and stood naked before all eyes: It was Dawn, radiant with youth and life. Never before had her equal existed, neither in the world of the gods nor among men nor in the abyss of the fundaments of the universe among the serpents of the nether waters whose flood bears the world. The waves of her blue-black hair shimmered like a peacock's feathers, and her long, dark, arched brows resembled the bows of the god of love, and her eyes like dark lotus blossoms had the lively, questioning expression of the gazelle. Her moon-round countenance was like a purple lotus flower, and her steep breasts seemed to strive upward toward her chin; with their two dark points she could bewitch saints. Her body was slender like a spear shaft, and her soft thighs resembled the elephant's outstretched trunk. Her face sprinkled with fine pearls of sweat, she stood in the adornment of all her charms and laughed quietly. (*Ibid.*)

Full of desire for her, all present asked what was to fall to her lot when the world became manifest. Brahma again looked into his heart, incubated his depths, and

> from his soul sprang up a magnificent being, a man resplendent like golden dust, enticing and strong. Round and well-formed of limb, his chest broad like a folding-door and adorned with a line of hair, with lively brows that met in the middle, he exuded the fragrance of flowers and resembled an elephant drunk with ardor. Tall and slim-hipped, he bore the sign of the fish in his banner and swung a bow of flowers and five flower arrows in his hands. (P. 253)

This god of love receives the task of enchanting men and women with his bow and arrow in order to affect the on-going creation of the world. Not even the gods will be able to withstand his arrows. "The goal of your arrows is the heart; to all breathing creatures thou shalt bring drunkenness and joy. These are your workings that drive forward the creation of the world" (*ibid.*).

The god of love, Kama, made himself invisible and prepared his bow and arrows of blossoms. Now he wanted to find out whether or not he could carry out his task, for here the wonderously beautiful woman stood before him. "He fitted a blossom arrow on the blossom cord and vigorously drew the bow. Intoxicating breezes began to blow, heavy with the scent of spring flowers, and spread delight" (p. 254). He enchanted them all; from the body of Brahma "all feelings and impulses with their involuntary gestures and forms of expression entered the light of day," and the woman answered with womanly movements: "feigned reticence and enamoured desire to please." The god of love was satisfied; he knew now that he could fulfill his task in this world. "And a marvelous feeling of himself completely filled him."

Meanwhile Shiva awoke from his self-absorption, and as he caught sight of Brahma and his retinue in their blissful condition, he broke out in laughter. Shiva's appearance caused Brahma "to divide his world": His true nature appeared beside the one transformed by the god of love. In anger—or is it shame?—Brahma curses the god of love. He releases "the shapes of desire" and squeezes his passion out his pores. Thus arise the spirits of the departed, the ancestor spirits who demand sacrifice. Strangled lust is expressed visibly in spirits of the dead. But afterward Brahma retracts the curse on Kama.

The other gods strive to purify their senses. From the sweat of flowing desire dripping from Daksha, the oldest lord of creatures, there arises a majestic woman, gleaming like gold, her slender limbs radiant. He calls her Rati, meaning "loveplay."

Meanwhile Shiva's laughter still rings in Brahma's ears, and Brahma feels insulted and perplexed because Shiva in his self-absorption sees no woman; indeed, Shiva regards desire for women as something inferior. Brahma says to himself, "How shall the unfolding of the world be propelled, and its duration and its destruction, if Shiva takes no wife?" (Thus the personal insult is already rationalized and reinterpreted as a cosmic problem.) Nevertheless it is clear to him that, should Shiva remain distant from the round of life, "devoid of every passion," he will be good only for his yoga. While Brahma is contemplating these thoughts, he sees the god of love happily united with his Rati and gives him the task of infatuating Shiva so that he, too, "with blissful heart will take himself a wife."

Let his weapon, the love god says, be woman: "Create me a woman that will delight Shiva when I have aroused his longing." (Such precision: first the longing, then the content of the longing!) "Thereupon the creator of the worlds immersed himself in inner contemplation on the intention, 'I will create the most bewitching woman', but from the breath he exhaled during his contemplation there arose, with a wind of blossoms, spring" (p. 262). With the help of Spring, the god of love was supposed to enchant the god Shiva, but in his spirit Brahma wants to bring to life a woman who will enchant Shiva.

Brahma takes counsel with his spiritual sons and with Daksha. They come to the conclusion that none other than the great Maya herself, who constitutes the entire world—she, the "drunkenness of the dream of yoga, birthing the world"—could bewitch Shiva. With sacrifices Daksha is supposed to persuade the "holy substance of all forms" to be born as his daughter so that she will become Shiva's wife.

Daksha "placed her in his heart and concentrated his fervor in glowing asceticism in order bodily to behold the mother of the world with his eyes. . . . Immersed completely in inner contemplation of the divine energy which consists of the universe, he passed the time" (p. 263). This period of time corresponds precisely to the incubation phase, which, according to creativity studies, accompanies every creative process.

In perfect concentration, Brahma also praises the nourishing mother of the world, Maya, for 36,000 years. "All divine women are her manifestation, foremost the great goddesses: Lakshmi, goddess of good fortune, the wife of Vishnu; Sarasvati, the flowing wise speech of sacred revelations and traditions, who is Brahma's spouse" (p. 272). He addresses them: "Thou are pure spirit, highest bliss of beings, art the highest being and strength of all creatures, art desire and satisfaction, art pure light of heaven which illuminates the self-constraint of *samsara*, and for ever and ever as darkness thou overshadowest the world" (p. 273). When after 36,000 years he has not turned his essence away from Maya, she appears to him, dark and slender, with flowing hair, standing on her lion; "For what have you worshipped me? Say what you want; when I appear bodily, your success is certain." Brahma laments to her that Shiva, the lord of the spirits, walks alone, but if he takes no wife, creation cannot continue, and only she can charm him. He urgently implores her to cast a spell on Shiva, and in the form of the sorceress Kali, Maya is ready to be born as the daughter of Daksha in order to become Shiva's spouse.

But how Maya was to become Shiva's spouse proved to be problematic. The god of love admitted that all of his attempts to enchant Shiva had been unsuccessful: all the joys of spring, all the fond dallyings that lovers had displayed before Shiva had not been able to awaken a single spark of desire in him. Thereupon Brahma commanded the god of love to devote only one fourth of the day to the other creatures and three fourths of the day to seducing Shiva.

After Daksha had ardently venerated the goddess, she appeared to him and told him she would become his daughter and Shiva's beloved. Daksha returned home and began, without intercourse with a woman, to form creatures in himself: "Immersed in himself, he shaped forms that entered the world palpably from the depths of his soul." Then he took a wife, and when the "first image of desire from his soul fell on her, she conceived the goddess Maya."

The girl was born and grew up quickly. She was named Sati or Shakti, meaning the "perfect one" or "she who is." As a child she drew Shiva's picture daily. When she had grown out of childhood, she began, at her mother's bidding, to worship Shiva with night vigils, sacrificial offerings, and contemplation; for twelve months she lived in devotion dedicated to the god.

Brahma now believed that the time had come to draw Shiva's attention to the woman longing for him. When the phase in which Shakti worshiped Shiva in pure meditation was ending, Brahma betook himself "with his divine strength and spouse Savitri to Shiva on the Himalaya," and Vishnu appeared with his spouse, Lakshmi. When Shiva, the "divine ascetic," saw the two couples, "a budding longing for wife and marriage" seized him. He asked the reason of their visit.

Brahma replied: For the sake of the gods, for the sake of the universe we two are come. I am the creative ground of the world, Vishnu the ground of its duration, but thou bringest about the end of creatures. In the counterplay of our powers we depend upon one another and must work together; otherwise the world cannot be. If thou always remainst distant from the world, harnessed in yoga, barren of desire and disgust, thou canst not fulfill thy part of the course of the world.

If we three with our gestures do not work against each other, why do we have three separate bodies, different from the goddess Maya? In our true essences we are indeed one, only in our effects are we different. We are one single divinity, separated from each other into a trinity, and thus the divine power that moves us is threefold in the form of the goddesses Savitri and Lakshmi and the goddess of twilight, each according to the effects that she works upon the course of the world. Woman is the root from which desires arise; from possessing the beautiful woman arise desire and madness. (pp. 278–80)

Shiva let himself be persuaded and asked Brahma to show him the woman who could "share his most sublime vision with him." And Brahma told him it was Shakti, Daksha's daughter, who consumed herself in passion for him. Now the moment had come in which the god of love could approach him with the goddess of desire; he approached Shiva and "commanded Spring to exercise her charms on him."

It was a year since Shakti had taken her vow; Shiva appeared to her and told her that her vow had greatly pleased him; he wanted to grant her whatever she wanted. Of course he knew what moved her heart, but he wanted her to say it. However, she was ashamed and could not say what she had wanted ever since she had been a girl. The god of love saw Shiva's vulnerability: the wish to make a woman like Shakti speak of her longing for him. "Then he struck Shiva's heart with the arrow that awakens excitement." Excitedly Shiva gazed at the maiden and forgot the spiritual contemplation of the highest essence. Then the god of love struck him once again. Shakti was about to overcome her shyness and ask Shiva to grant her wish when he called out again and again: "Be my wife!" "Delicate laughter and loving gestures betrayed her feelings to the god, the deportment of love inspired them both."

"Go to my father and take me from his hand," she said as he repeated, "Be my wife!" Shakti hurried home to her parents, but Shiva retired to his hermitage and "in pain at the parting from it gave himself fully to its inner image." But he also recalled Brahma's admonition to take a wife; now all his thought turned toward Brahma, and "swift as thought he came through the ethers on his cart drawn by swans." Shiva had no more urgent wish than that Brahma should quickly arrange with Shakti's father the details of the wedding. Brahma did so and summoned his spiritual sons to accompany Shiva.

> Garbed in a tiger skin, a serpent slung as the brahmin's cord about his shoulders and hips, the god mounted his mighty steer; the sickle of the young moon in his hair cast a pale radiance over him. Noisily his multitudes (lesser and fantastic copies of him cast into the atmosphere by the tremendous force of his scintillating presence) exulted about him. . . . All the gods approached in ceremonious procession to accompany the bridegroom; the blessed and celestial women came with music and dance. The god of love appeared bodily with his retinue of feelings, delighting and enchanting Shiva. Round about the heavens were clear and bright; fragrant winds blew; every flower stood in blossoming splendor; every creature breathed health, and the suffering healed as Shiva, celebrated with music by all the gods, approached Daksha's dwelling. Swans, wild geese, and peacocks uttered sweet calls of joy as if they were accompanying him. (p. 283)

At Vishnu's bidding, Shiva immersed himself again in the inner contemplation that he had forgotten because of Shakti, and in his inner vision he again saw the entire creation: He saw a lonely mountain peak where he and Shakti were entwined in love; he saw how Shakti "released her own body" and arose again as the daughter of the Himalaya; he witnessed the birth of her son. But he also saw how Brahma entered Vishnu's body and how Vishnu's form dissolved "into the highest essence, which is pure light, blissful perception and knowledge." He saw the unity and multiplicity of the world, the unfolding, the sustaining, and the end.

When Shiva reemerged from his contemplation, his soul immediately flew to Shakti. He lifted Shakti up onto his steer Nandi and departed amidst the jubilation of the gods, demons, and essences. Once he reached the Himalaya, he sent all away, and the god and the goddess enjoyed their love for a long time. The god of love came to them and spring to the earth, and Shiva and Shakti found great pleasure in each other.

When the hot season approached, Shakti lamented that they had no house to shelter them, yet Shiva said, smiling, that in his wanderings through the wilderness he needed no house. They thus spent the hot season together under shade trees. When the rainy season came, Shakti again asked Shiva to build her a house. But Shiva said, "I have nothing with which to build a house; a tiger skin covers my loins, serpents are my ornament." And Shakti was ashamed for him. Instead of providing a house, he lifted her up above the clouds and remained united with her there until the rainy season had passed.

Shiva's heart was completely filled by Shakti, and he was untiring in his demonstrations of love and ardor. He could think of nothing other than her; he no longer knew the highest essence nor contemplation. Shakti's gaze hung ceaselessly on the great god's countenance, and Shiva's eyes were fixed on her face: "The inexhaustible stream of his passion nourished the tree of their love, so that it spread out its crown in their union without end."

Possibilities and Problems in the Shiva-Shakti Fantasy of Relationship

Brahma, the creator god and accordingly the model of every creative person, brings forth the world through imagination; by concentrating on his own depths, the images of the world arise in him and assume form. This creation myth, in which Shiva is led into love, demonstrates the importance of inner contemplation—that is, imagining the beloved person—and hence the importance of the fantasy of relationship. The god of love incites the fantasy, but it cannot develop without participants.

This myth also beautifully demonstrates how, through the creation of the god of love, events among gods and humans become unpredictable, as a spontaneous and uncontrollable dynamism enters life. The myth suggests that without love, the entire cycle of becoming, enduring, and passing away could not continue.

Shiva is initially depicted in the image of the god who is self-contained and unexpressive. He is passive energy, whereas Shakti, the personification of Maya, the mother goddess, is active energy. When Shiva encounters Shakti, love, ardor, passion, and a tremendous intensity of life are released in him; he also releases the same feelings in her.

The ideal of relationship that the two embody is, whether perceived or not, the guiding image of all love: the negation of separateness. Shiva and Shakti are everything to each other, and their relationship completely excludes the outside world. They live full of passion, in eternal embrace. In this eternal embrace they symbolize a wholeness that transcends their individual beings and everyday life. They thus present an image of ideal love, and this image is encountered again and again when we are seized by love. We are constantly led away from such ideal images by the force of reality. We all wish that these moments of transcendence produced by love would endure, as they do for Shiva and Shakti; only those of us more attuned to reality perhaps dare to question whether such an idealized state of love might not get tedious.

Shiva and Shakti do not really have a history of relationship with each other. We learn only that Shiva's heart is completely filled by Shakti, that he could think only of her, and that for her he forgot the highest essence and contemplation. We learn that Shakti's gaze hung incessantly on Shiva while his eyes were fixed on her face, and we are told that "the inexhaustible stream of his passion nourished the tree of their love [and] its crown spread out in their union without end." This is not a depiction of the history of their relationship but rather of their immersion in each other.

Shakti tries twice to create an additional realm for relating: She would like to have a house for the summer and one for protection from the rain. Shiva rejects these wishes because to him they represent separation; he would like to be everything to her. Their fusion is not threatening to either of them, for although they are entirely engrossed in each other, they cannot lose themselves because both want the same thing, at least initially. Shakti's wishes for shelter, however, suggest separation and parting.

Their eternal embrace symbolizes the human wish to overcome and to deny responsibility for our individuality. In a loving union individuals may overcome their separateness, but only for a time. Even the two divine partners have problems with separation. For couples whose ideal of relationship corresponds to the divine marriage of Shiva and Shakti, the problems of separation eventually emerge. Fundamental questions must be faced (Who am I? Who are you? What do I want? What does my fate want of me and of my relationship to you?), and the problem of parting from a partner must be confronted.

In the myth of Shiva and Shakti, it is Shiva who is somewhat more fearful of parting. He reacts very strongly to his first parting from Shakti, and in an attempt to deny his fears, he plunges himself into her image and persuades Brahma to speed up the process of their union. When they are together, Shiva initially rejects each of Shakti's attempts at delimitation. Shakti can tolerate separation somewhat better than Shiva; she is the first to go her own way. But before focusing on the separation issues involved in this myth, I would like to quote from Guy de Maupassant's story, "Indiscretion," which contains parallels to the myth of Shiva and Shakti:

> When they slept, they dreamt about each other; when they were awake, they thought of each other. They belonged to each other with body and soul and thirsted for each other long before they were conscious of it. After their wedding they had paradise on earth, initially in sensuously unfettered delirium, then in ardent, blissfully delicate touch, caresses without equal, in ever new and ever more daring demonstrations of their passion. Every glance was hot desire, every gesture an echo of glowing nights. Gradually, however, they began, without admitting it, to get bored. Certainly they still loved each other! But in this love there was no longer anything new.[2]

The relationship described in this passage suggests that of Shiva and Shakti, but de Maupassant is depicting human beings, who are subject to boredom. In de Maupassant's story, the remedy to boredom is the man's telling his wife love stories from his earlier life. This action allows the partners to differentiate each other, and a degree of separation takes place. Maupassant's story clearly expresses how the most fervent love exhausts itself if separation (the opposite of union) is not acknowledged. Two persons who love ardently and exclusively must preserve their individuality if their love is to survive.

Fear of separation also concerned the thirty-five-year-old artist mentioned at the beginning of this chapter who avoided relationships because of his fear. He also feared that fascination with another could so possess him that he might completely lose himself in a relationship. What he wants and fears in a love relationship can be experienced intrapsychically if he works creatively. And just as a love relationship might fascinate him too much, perhaps the fascination emanating from a creative process might be unendurable for him. Whether or not he could really endure, however, also depends on his ego structure. There are people who, if they belong totally to another, also lose themselves completely and become too dependent on their partner.

The relationship of a married couple between thirty and forty who believed themselves to be enlightened and modern offers another example of a Shiva-Shakti constellation. They knew something about the "overcharged dyadic relationship"[3] and had accordingly agreed that although they would not wantonly seek other lovers, they would not forbid each other extramarital relationships. But they had agreed that under all conditions their relationship had to remain very special. The husband met a woman who greatly stimulated him and awoke in him some of his creative potential. He openly told his wife about his feelings for the other woman. She responded with reproaches, accusations, and suspicions. He did not know how to justify himself; since nothing had transpired sexually with the other woman, he thought that he would have no reason to reproach himself. His wife, however, did not believe him. She felt devalued, and plagued by self-doubt. She said, "As a woman, I'm not enough for you; I don't bring into our marriage what you need." All this couple's previous thoughts about the "overcharged dyadic relationship" and the impossibility of one person being everything for another were now meaningless. Eventually, however, the woman who had inspired the man became a friend of the wife's as well and was highly valued by both of them.

Some time later the wife read a book by Erich Fromm. She was fascinated and enlivened by his work and began to speak of him often; she also pondered what sort of person Fromm could have been. Her husband reacted by criticizing Fromm and mustering all possible and impossible arguments against him. One day his wife disarmed him by saying, "But you really wouldn't be jealous of a book, would you?" He did not want that, of course, and suddenly recognized that he was actually competing with Fromm.

This couple had consciously chosen an ideal of comradely togetherness and had nursed a fantasy of "being everything to each other" without being aware of it. In the desire for complete togetherness is hidden the hope of attaining wholeness, which is probably only experienced when we intrapsychically perceive images such as Shiva and Shakti, who represent the union of possibilities in our own soul.

For this couple the separation from each other implied that the fantasy of complete togetherness was endangered, and both of them felt abandoned, anxious, and in need of regaining their wholeness. Perhaps we make it too simple for ourselves when we reproach our partner for newly initiated relationships instead of asking what such actions mean in terms of our relationship and what developmental steps it demands of the individual partner.

Experiencing wholeness in a relationship is achieved only in fateful hours; apart from those moments, the struggle to attain wholeness becomes the most personal task for each of us. Wholeness is a gift that cannot be won by force; it is continually stimulated by one's partner, usually when we see ourselves as separated from him or her and are conscious that wholeness can never be a gift we get from another. Reluctance to separate from another may also mean that one does not yet want to abandon the fantasy of wholeness associated with the relationship.

It is important for couples whose conscious fantasy of relationship is a very intimate one to consider whether or not there may be a Shiva-Shakti fantasy at work. A couple's conscious fantasy would then always have to be compared with the unconscious fantasy of belonging totally to each other, and problems that arise would have to be examined to see whether or not this hidden wish is also a factor. This means that every parting, not only a final separation or a divorce, would have to be experienced and pondered, and painful feelings could not simply be recast as reproaches, prohibitions, or conditions; they would have to be understood as signs that neither person in the couple can expect his or her wholeness to come completely from the other. Wherever a Shiva-Shakti fantasy of relationship is active, the theme of parting is important.

The following example will illustrate what it might mean to see and experience Shiva and Shakti as a couple in one's own psyche, that is, to perceive them as intrapsychic images.

A thirty-four-year-old man said of himself that he was on a "disillusionment course." By this he meant that he now finally wanted to see things as clearly as possible—as they are, not as he desired them to be. He felt that he finally had to stop recasting events according to his own wishes. In his marriage he was also endeavoring to dismantle idealizations and to demand that his wife no longer idealize him. He had the following dream:

> I am observing a sculpture of Shiva and Shakti. The two of them, in their interaction, appear perfect. Even the division of space is right; each of them occupies exactly the right space vis-à-vis the other. Fascinated, I contemplate the sculpture. The figures step out of the frame; they become flesh and blood, and dance before me. The harmony, beauty, and wholeness seize me; I am smitten and moved. Very gradually they disappear.

He awoke with the feeling of knowing what wholeness is and with the pain of having lost it again. These feelings of wholeness and longing accompanied him for days. He could summon the feelings at any time and immerse himself fully in them. He also knew that something like this cannot be lived in projection: "I have to seek this feeling wherever I can find it."

This dream clearly expresses how the images of Shiva and Shakti and the existential feelings accompanying them can evoke a sense of wholeness in a person if they are experienced in one's own psyche. The dreamer also expressed his pain that this experience did not continue, these feelings of wholeness are transient and have their own rhythm. Life is perhaps a striving for balance, not a state of equilibrium.

The Longing for Love Without Words

The Shiva-Shakti fantasy of relationship is connected to the longing for speechless love, that is, a love that needs no words.[4] The longing to love an unknown, marvelous person whom one does not need to understand verbally, who perhaps comes from another planet, and for whom one also remains the beautiful, mysterious stranger is a common fantasy. One's own image in this fantasy of relationship is also that of the mysterious, unknown stranger; these images call for discovery and exploration, but also for love.

Such a fantasy frequently involves going to a foreign city in a mysterious country, meeting a person, and being fascinated at first sight by that person. The same thing happens to the stranger, if possible with somewhat greater intensity and yearning. Because neither needs to speak the same language as the other, the two agree without words to love. This love is an experience of bliss—a dialogue of bodies without involving language—enveloped in the magic of the mysterious. These fantasies usually break off at this point because the mysterious would become more familiar, and the condition of being unknown could not be repeated. In *Paar und Sprache* [*Couple and Language*] Leisi mentions such a fantasy and uses the expressions "mute love" and "love without words"[5] to describe it.

In this fantasy of love without words is expressed the longing to be understood without having to speak. This wish plays a great role in many relationships: The magnitude of the love is sometimes measured by how many of one's own wishes one's partner guesses or sees in one's eyes without their being stated. Sometimes the hope for this nonverbal understanding is so great that one's partner is supposed to guess the wishes that one does not even sense oneself.

This wish for a love without words is part of the idea that love grants sight, an idea that is not in itself incorrect. Although love does endow us with a clairvoyance of sorts, an ability to see possibilities of development, it definitely requires our language in order to acknowledge everyday wishes and needs. In this wish to be understood without words, there also lies hidden a longing for divine love such as that shared by Shiva and Shakti. Such a state of union needs no words, for words can create separations and misunderstandings; words reveal that two persons are not nearly as close in their wishes and views as they would like to be or pretend to be. In love without words, the separative factor that speech introduces falls away, and the communication of bodies becomes much more important. In such a state of love, people are undisguised in relation to each other.

When the image of the mysterious stranger strongly influences the fantasy, the longing for the entirely foreign is also present. These mysterious strangers can be seen as a longing for something strange or foreign in our own soul, and the longing must not be too quickly ensnared in our accustomed language or it would rapidly be reduced to the habitual.

In his play, *As the War Ended*, Max Frisch depicts this love without words. He is concerned with showing that a love in which the two lovers cannot under-stand each other verbally can be lived "without fear and without pretense," be-cause they can be closer to each other. At work here is a Shiva-Shakti fantasy of relationship, an ideal that can never be attained. In his play, Frisch depicts a "normal" relationship that the character Agnes maintains with her husband (who is hidden in the cellar). Their relationship involves the questions: What do you say to each other when you have been apart so long? What do you keep to yourself? What can you absolutely not tell each other? Frisch confronts her with a relationship to a Russian colonel quartered in her apartment whom she visits each evening, with whom she falls in love, and who for her is the extraordinary man who understands her without words. Frisch has Agnes say the following:

> If you hadn't come, Stepan, I wouldn't have known that that exists: that I can be like I am with you, without fear and deception, *so real, so absolute*! Do you feel that? I'm telling you things I've never been able to tell anybody: you hear me, Stepan, and yet it all remains a secret. Look, even I don't know who you are. Only that we love each other. And then you are simply there: you are everything that I could want. How do I deserve it? . . . And then, you know, there are never any lies between us.[6]

No fear, no pretense, no lies—this is what Agnes experiences as new. But the Russian colonel leaves when her husband intrudes on their idyllic relationship. Love without words can thus only be lived for a short time. In Frisch's play the total, ideal love is linked with the love between mysterious strangers, and it is understood as the experience of a genuine, deep surrender to love, from which the everyday world is almost entirely excluded.

Parting as Problem

In the fantasy of relationship represented in the myth of Shiva and Shakti, the feeling of wholeness granted by the other's love is experienced very intensely. Lovers who idealize this sense of wholeness and exclusivity see others as dis-turbances to their relationship, and hence these lovers are also often excluded by their contemporaries. Separation, which implies loosening the eternal embrace, is experienced as loss of wholeness; lovers seek to avoid such loss and thus close themselves off even more from the outside world.

The myth addresses the problem of parting. In this myth, parting is associated with being excluded from the world. Daksha, Shakti's mundane father, wanted to celebrate a great sacrificial feast for the salvation of all beings. He invited everyone except Shiva and Shakti. He considered Shiva unworthy of participating in the feast because he carried in his hands a skull, which was a sign of his destructive, disintegrative side, and Shakti was considered sullied by her husband's flaw.

When one of Shakti's sisters told the couple of the sacrificial feast and asked them why they had not been invited, Shakti was so angry at her father that she wanted to utter a curse to turn him into ashes. But she remembered that she had made an agreement with him: She would forsake her body and this life if he should ever fail to show her adequate respect. And so she was swallowed up by her primal form but reminded herself that the purpose for which she had become Shiva's wife had not been fulfilled, since Shiva had not yet had a son with her. She intended to keep her promise and thus decided to die and return again as the child of Meneka, the wife of Himalaya; she would then become Shiva's wife again and bear him a son. Thus she "dreamed into herself." Again a rage overcame her, and "she closed all nine gates of the senses and of the body in yoga, held her breath and burst her body."

In this myth, the impulses toward parting always originated with Shakti. Through her voluntary death, she leaves Shiva because of the affront of having been excluded, that is, because of an idea. Or does she go because the relationship in this form can no longer be lived? To be sure, she makes up her mind how and in what form she will return. It is interesting that in the eternal embrace there was no opportunity to have a child; the eternal embrace is therefore not fruitful symbolically either. Although Shakti's act of parting is a radical one, it must be remembered that Indian philosophy views death as a departure from one form and a return in another (as in Shakti's death and return as Meneka's daughter).

Nevertheless, when he hears of the death of his wife, Shiva mourns intensely; following the great love, he must come to terms with the great parting. Through the example of Shiva, this myth also demonstrates a process of mourning and surviving a loss.

Shiva concluded his devotions and rode homeward on his white steer Nandi; there he found Shakti lying dead on the ground. "But his love did not believe appearances. Again and again he caressed her and asked, 'Why are you sleeping? What put you to sleep?'" Shiva's first reaction is not to accept Shakti's death. Following this first phase of denial in the mourning process,[7] Shiva experiences the eruption of chaotic emotions: He arises in his burning emotions as an all-consuming fire. From his eyes, nose, and mouth fiery flames shoot out, meteors roar forth from him. Incandescent with rage, he approaches the area of Daksha's sacrificial feast. Infinite rage seizes him when he sees those assembled, and he sends Virabhadra, the lion-faced "Lord of the Hosts" who personifies Shiva's rage, to break into the holy precinct and destroy it.

Vishnu fights Virabhadra in a fierce battle; only when Vishnu has hurled Virabhadra to the ground does Shiva himself enter the fray. Vishnu becomes invisible and disappears. On the sacrifice ground he burns the fire to ashes, but the sacrifice transforms itself into a gazelle that Shiva now wants to catch. He sets out after it, then suddenly finds himself again before Shakti's corpse.

Shiva, like a mortal in mourning, is overcome by anger and thoughts of revenge. Blinded by rage, Shiva forgets the departed, and only his relationship to the sacrifice again brings him back to Shakti's corpse and thus emotionally to his pain: "Gruesome pain overwhelmed him, and he sobbed wildly like a common mortal."

The love god hears him lamenting and approaches with Love's Delight and with Spring; the love god strikes Shiva in the heart with an arrow and causes a complete confusion of feelings in him: "Although overwhelmed with grief, Shiva became wild with longing for love; inundated with suffering he behaved as mad with love. Torn by the conflicting feelings, he began to rage; now he threw himself to the ground, now he jumped up and rushed away, now he knelt by Shakti's corpse and stared at it, lost in thought."[8] As if it were not enough that Shiva is overpowered by rage, anger, and pain, the feelings of love for the departed Shakti break forth anew and make him completely helpless; he is torn by conflicting emotions, as is every mortal mourner in this phase.

When Brahma sees Shiva's hot tears, he and the gods become anxious: If these tears fell on the earth, they could incinerate everything. They call on the planet Saturn for help; unable to contain the glowing fire, Saturn hurls it on the farthest mountain of the world. The mountain is not able to hold it, and the raging fire penetrates into the sea and becomes the "River Without Crossing," which surrounds the realm of the god of death. This myth is, of course, a creation myth, and it explains not only the origin of the world through love but the origin of death.

Shiva now had to tear himself away, step by step, from the departed. I have described this phase in the human mourning process as that of seeking, finding, and parting.[9] Shiva takes Shakti's corpse on his shoulders and, crazed with pain, runs toward the East with it. Though he can no longer love the living Shakti, he will still not part from her corpse. In the process of mourning, the mourner, having everywhere "sought" the departed, again finds and wants to continue living with him or her, even if with memories instead of with the living person. But one must take leave of this phase, too—even from the memories of the deceased—or one is lost to the world of the living.

In the myth, the gods knew this truth. They are worried that as long as Shiva holds Shakti's body, it will never decay, and the eternal transformation of all life will be arrested. Brahma, Vishnu, and Saturn therefore stole into Shakti's body and made it fall to the ground piece by piece, but everywhere that a part of the goddess fell to the ground, it was revered under another name.

Shiva must let go of Shakti, piece by piece, but he does not do this voluntarily; rather, he is robbed of her—by the power of the gods or by the nature of fate that knows eternal transformation. So that the life process can continue, each of Shakti's parts becomes a memorial to the goddess and permits her to continue to play a role in the life of mortals. Shiva must suffer through this process of transformation. Where Shakti's head fell to the ground, Shiva stopped and observed the event, overwhelmed by pain. Even if this process of mourning serves life, it is dreadful to experience.

The gods approach Shiva to console him. When "he saw them approach, pain and shame overwhelmed him. Before their eyes he turned to stone and in his illusion and pain of love he hardened into a great lingam."[10] The lingam in Indian religion is the symbol of the procreative capacity. In becoming rigid, Shiva manifests his most unique essence, namely, as symbol of a creative, procreative god. Does this suggest that when we are petrified by pain and shame, we are thrown back on our basic nature, which we must reflect upon?[11]

In this phase, the gods ask Shiva to abandon his pain and to recollect himself as the highest being. The gods' concerns are essential ones: In the process of mourning there comes the time when one must sacrifice one's pain, for it is often the pain that takes the place of the deceased person. To be able to continue to live, the pain must be abandoned. But we can sacrifice the pain—and the word *sacrifice* is very important here—only if we first recollect ourselves. Just as Shiva must remember himself as the highest being, perhaps as mourners we must call to mind our own special possibilities, the actualization of which is our task in life.

Shiva cannot immediately recall his "highest being." He still needs Brahma's encouragement and is continually advised by Brahma to let go of his pain and his rage. Brahma tells him that he will possess Shakti again but in a different form. Shiva asks Brahma to accompany him until he can emerge from his pain— a hint that we mortal mourners need a companion, too, until we can release our pain. Brahma leads Shiva away from the site of his loss and up to the peaks of the Himalaya. They come to a small lake of solitude. Beside the waters of this lake Shiva can again compose himself, and he lingers there in meditation until the goddess Parvati, daughter of the mountain king Himalaya and his wife Meneka, fetches him from his solitude, and they again live with one another.

In this new life form, Shiva and Shakti have a son together, as Shakti had predicted. Perhaps we can understand this to mean that only when we have lived through love *and* parting can love become truly creative. The myth teaches that nothing can remain as it is and as we wish it to be in the moments of the greatest love and intimacy with another person. It suggests that parting from each other becomes a fundamental problem precisely when we want to belong completely to one another. Lovers may have to endure such pain as Shiva's not only at the time of an ultimate loss—the death of a beloved person—but at the time of every smaller parting within a relationship.

It is important to be familiar with these phases of mourning and to withstand them, for they are also a part of love. Otherwise there would remain only the attempt to cancel out the repeatedly necessary partings, which can also enrich a relationship. By denying the inevitable small partings, the great parting usually has to be sought so that the partners can again recollect their life tasks.

The Shiva-Shakti myth expresses a basic idea about human love: Love involves the feeling of wholeness but also the necessity and pain of separation. Couples must repeatedly part from each other and live as individuals; again and again they must let go of the wholeness they attained. By enduring the process of mourning that is not to be separated from the experience of love, each of us is thrown back on ourselves, and from a new understanding and awareness of ourselves, each of us can experience a more creative and fertile love.

Because the relationship between Shiva and Shakti expresses basic truths about human love and separation, it can be regarded as a fundamental fantasy of every relationship. But how does one deal with such a fascination in the real world? The couple who had wanted to develop an equitable relationship but who discovered only through their jealousies that each had very different fantasies had to recognize that there was a great difference between their ideal (the Shiva-Shakti fantasy) and their conscious conviction (equitable partnership). The dilemma between the ideal and the reality of a relationship cannot be resolved; the reality of the relationship can only be compared, again and again, to the ideal. The problems that arise in a relationship reveal the ideals each person aspires to individually or as part of the couple.

This particular couple had to learn that jealousy was an important aspect of their relationship, despite their attempts to minimize it. They had to learn that jealousy is not merely the expression of a desire to possess and of an inability to let go of one's mate but that it can also be the sign that the relationship is in danger. Naturally I am not talking about persons who are so jealous that they suspiciously watch their partner's every move, who really want to have their partner entirely for themselves alone, and who have never learned to be alone, to mourn, or to trust the possibility of renewed closeness within an existing relationship.

This couple had to learn that no one person can be everything for another. Stimulation from outside the relationship, including from new persons in one's life, can enrich and transform the relationship.

It is not always so simple to part from one's ideals, to mourn, and to open oneself to new people and impulses. In further examining the case of the thirty-five-year-old man who did not want to enter a fascinating relationship, we can explore the ideal of a Shiva-Shakti relationship from another perspective.

Chapter 3

PYGMALION:

The Longing To Shape a Partner
in One's Own Image

"O gods, if gods have power unlimited,
This only is my prayer, that I may wed"—
To say: "my ivory maid," he did not dare;
But turned it thus: "my maiden ivory-fair."
—Ovid

My Fair Lady

Herbert, the thirty-five-year-old "bourgeois artist," as he called himself, was able to recognize that a Shiva-Shakti ideal decisively influenced his fantasies of relationship. He was aware that he could not enter into any relationship, particularly with a woman who really fascinated him, because of his fear of separation. We also linked his fear of overstimulation in his creative work with the intrapsychic aspect of the union of Shiva and Shakti, that is, with the experience of wholeness that he both yearned for and feared. It was unthinkable to him to relinquish his ideal of relationship, especially after we had talked about it, but he knew with equal certainty that this ideal was not to be realized. He felt himself to be blocked.

He was always complaining about his boring girl friend. When I suggested that he had consciously chosen a woman who bored him, he revealed that he had fantasized "making something" out of this woman so that he could then love her. In this way he would have a great love and would still control the situation. He was reminded of the musical *My Fair Lady*. "I would like to draw out of a woman everything that seems to me worthwhile and that I want in order to be able to live with her. At first she must be boring. But I can't stand it when she adores me enough to let me shape her. That probably isn't possible any longer, anyway, because of the women's movement."

It seemed to me that a new fantasy of relationship was addressed here. I asked him how he envisioned himself in this fantasy in order to see his part in the relationship more clearly and to recognize what unconscious elements responded to the image of the woman he could shape. Of himself he said: "I would see myself like God—with limitations, of course. This way perhaps you could eliminate the flaws in creation . . . [and perhaps also magnify them]." He also said that he saw himself as very creative in such situations, for he could shape someone according to his own ideas; he could "put a personality on her."

In this fantasy of relationship he saw himself as a person who, in his creativity, resembled God. That sounds rather arrogant, but it suggests that a deep longing for creativity has taken form in a fantasy that is very closely connected with his innermost nature and potential. To be sure I understood his fantasy clearly—and to determine viability of his new ideal—I asked him what sort of role there would be for the woman in this relationship: "She would be sure to please me; she could admire and could love me, and I would certainly love her. Then we

could belong to each other completely, without anything coming between us.
I would envision her such that she would never part from me."

Although this appears to be a new fantasy of relationship, it is actually another
expression of the Shiva-Shakti ideal. This man's role at first seems to be essentially different from Shiva's: He intends to shape his mate. This fantasy is of
the greatest importance to his creative process, for by fantasizing a woman—
forming her in fantasy—he also fantasizes himself in the act of shaping; he creates
intrapsychically a union of masculine and feminine that greatly satisfies him
and endows him with the creative power of giving form. It was clear to him,
however, that such an ideal relationship was not viable: "This fantasy stimulated
me immensely; I'd like to live that way, but of course it's not possible; a woman
is, after all, an autonomous person, not a piece of wax."

This man's ideal of a relationship in which two people completely belong to
and understand each other is reminiscent of the relationship between Shiva
and Shakti. In Herbert's fantasy, however, he imagined himself as the creator
and was thus more active than Shiva, even if their "goal" was the same: to love
someone without limitation or the necessity of separation.

Wanting to shape one's partner is a fantasy that is familiar to most people,
although it may rarely be admitted or predominate in such an extreme form.
Most people are satisfied if they exorcise their partner of some annoying tendencies or strengthen desired characteristics. Is this desire to transform another a
subtle educative process, a byproduct of love (for nothing transforms more than
love), or a creative act? Envisioning a partner's best possibilities and thus, enabling
that person to transcend his or her limitations is not the same as wanting to
shape a partner according to one's own wishes, but loving fantasies and concealed power drives are closely related. Which of them gains the upper hand in a
relationship depends on whether we really love and whether we can grant our
partner autonomy.

Pygmalion

The longing to transform one's partner is a common theme in literature.
Herbert had already referred to this theme in *My Fair Lady*, which seemed to him
to express his fantasy of relationship. The musical *My Fair Lady* is based on
George Bernard Shaw's comedy *Pygmalion*, which premiered in 1913. Briefly
summarized, the plot is as follows: Professor Higgins, a linguist and student of
dialects, takes note of the unusual language of a common flower vendor. Higgins
wants to make a lady of her, and this transformation is to come about through
her language. Eliza begins language lessons with him and makes great progress.
Higgins is also in love with her, but he does not admit it. Whether or not she will
be accepted into higher society—and that she can attain only by marriage—remains open. What is impressive is how Higgins appears as the new creator of
Eliza and how she lets herself be shaped. The comedy and the musical refer
to the saga of Pygmalion:

> And thanks to them Pygmalion, who beheld
> Their life of sin, by female faults repelled
> (Nature's too numerous gifts to woman's mind),
> Lived without wife, to single state resigned,
> And carved with wonderous skill and fashioned sure

A female form in ivory, snowy pure.
He gave his work such grace as never lit
On mortal maid, and fell in love with it.
She seemed a thing of flesh and blood to be
And held entranced by mere timidity.
Thus art veiled art, and by the illusion swayed,
Pygmalion loved the semblance of a maid.
If flesh it was or ivory he would try
By sense of touch, and still the truth deny.
He spoke to her and kissed her oft and thought
Each kiss returned; so strangely fancy wrought;
And when he held her in his arms, believed
The yielding flesh his fingers' dint received,
And feared to bruise it. Now with words he woos,
And now with gifts no maiden can refuse:
Bright beads, and birds, and flowers of varied hues,
Tears of the sun-god's daughters from their tree,
Lilies, and shells, and pebbles from the sea.
And then in garments gay her limbs he dressed,
With rings for fingers, sashes for her breast,
Necklace and earrings: all she well could wear
Yet seemed without her finery no less fair.
Then fabrics fine of richest hue he spread,
Dyed with the sells of Tyre, to make her bed;
And called her bride; and as of sense possessed,
On softest down her head was made to rest.
    And now the day was come, when Cypriotes all,
In praise of Venus, held high festival.
The incense smoked; and calves with necks of snow,
And horns new-gilt, had felt the slaughterer's blow.
Within the shrine, his offering duly paid,
Pygmalion thus with timid utterance prayed:
"O gods, if gods have power unlimited,
This only is my prayer, that I may wed"—
To say: "my ivory maid," he did not dare;
But turned it thus: "my maiden ivory-fair."
Venus, who, present there in golden pride,
Graced her own feast, knew what this prayer implied;
And soon in sign of heavenly grace, there came,
Thrice kindled in the air, a darting flame.
Pygmalion hastened home, and, bending o'er
To kiss his beauty, found her cold no more.
He kissed her once again, and touched her breast:
The ivory lost its hardness as he pressed,
And gave beneath his fingers, as wax
Of mount Hymettus in the sun grows lax,
And kneaded oft, from shape to shape will go,
And pliant to the hand by handling grow.
Amazed, in doubt and joy, he feared some cheat,
And clasped his idol with a lover's heat.—
'Twas flesh and blood, and, as he felt again,
Beneath his fingers leaped the pulsing vein.
Ah, now the Paphian youth, with formal phrase

Full-charged with gratitude, to Venus prays;
And now at last the lover's lip can greet,
With pressure fond, a lip not counterfeit.
The maiden too was conscious of the kiss,
And blushed, and raised her timid eyes to his;
And on her sight, as sense of vision woke,
At once the daylight and her lover broke.
When dawned the wedding-day, to join the pair,
Venus, whose work it was, was present there.
When nine moons waxed and waned, their daughter came,
Paphos, from whom the island has its name.[1]

Whereas Brahma catches sight of a woman and creates her in his imagination, Pygmalion sculpts a woman after his ideal. The myth of Pygmalion has not been particularly popular among women; he considered women faulty, and none pleased him. He could not find a woman with whom to share his fantasy of relationship because his ideal image does not coincide with reality; he would deprive a woman of her autonomy. Pygmalion is a man who forms his fantasy to such a degree that it comes to life; even if the woman appears beautiful, perfect, passive, and empty, he remains the creator. But behind this fantasy of relationship is the longing to be able really to love a woman.

If we view the Pygmalion fantasy as a wish for a possible union of the feminine and the masculine in the psyche of a man or a woman, then other aspects become visible, and the situation can be seen with less prejudice.

The wish to "make" something of one's mate is certainly one of our ideals of relationship. Lovers frequently praise their partners by saying such things as, "You have gotten more beautiful because of our love" or "You have gained a lot of courage and self-confidence through our love." Both men and women use such joyous expressions; we feel good when our love encourages a person's growth. Like Pygmalion, lovers may also desire to see their partners dress in ways that best suit them, and this desire is another expression of the wish to make something of the other. This wish may also involve wanting to "save" the partner or find what is deemed the "appropriate" life for him or her. This ideal of wanting to make something of one's partner, of revealing that person's finest qualities, is based on the lover's objective recognition—and not only on the lover's subjective fantasy—of the beloved's potential. A lover helps a partner develop his or her potential through the loving trust in their relationship.

When a beloved's perceived potential is too slow in its realization, we are sometimes tempted to help it develop. When this happens, the beloved is no longer permitted the autonomy to grow freely; instead, the beloved is squeezed into an image that conforms to our needs. In such a relationship, one's own pride and the satisfaction of one's needs supersede the well-being of one's mate.

In the frequently surprising developmental history of two persons, however, both are creator as well as creation. The problem of a Pygmalion fantasy is that one partner is creator and the other creation, instead of each being creator as well as creation. But Pygmalion and other lovers and would-be lovers want to be creators not only from a will to dominate but also from the desperate hope of finally being able to love someone whom they have made lovable. Even if we conceptualize Pygmalion and his wife as figures in *one* person—and, to be sure, in a situation where the feminine is shaped there remains an imbalance—the Pygmalion fantasy could only remain an interlude.

The Pygmalion story is sometimes criticized because it contains an implicit imbalance: A woman could not assume the role of Pygmalion in the same way that a man could. In his novel *Wovon du Traeumst* [*Whereof You Dream*], Horst Wolfram Geissler describes how a couple prompt each other to their greatest possible creative achievement through their work (through her he becomes a poet; she is an actress). In this novel it is the woman who causes the man, an assistant secretary in the department of justice, to take his poetic attempts seriously. The woman's former husband has the following conversation with her:

"You see, I'm not entirely certain whether or not the story of Pygmalion can simply be turned around."

"What does that mean?" Fen wanted to know.

". . . Look: I believe that the sculptor Pygmalion created such a beautiful image of woman that he fell in love with it. I also believe that the gods made the marble come to life as a favor to him, and that then the two of them lived together very happily. That may have happened, for I can imagine that the picture-pretty girl learned how to cook well and darn socks diligently and put flowers on the table. Because ultimately she had to thank the man that she had come to life."

"And?"

"But assume now that Pygmalion had not been a man but a woman. So this woman artist creates a statue of a man, and the story—turned completely around—goes on in precisely the same way."

"Ok. And?"

"Well," Peters said. "So far as I know men—I don't know! In any case, had the fellow been successfully brought to life, he probably would neither have cooked nor darned socks, and he wouldn't have put flowers on the table, either, but no later than the third day he would have slammed his fist on the table and roared 'Damn it anyway, where's the food? Is that nonsense going to go on for ever!'"

"And then?"

"Then?" . . . [Peters] asked. "I think that's enough. But Pygmalion—that nice, genial little woman would forthwith have raised her arms to the gods sobbing and implored them for support against this mad man, against this arrogant male creature, against this miserable character."

"And what would the gods do?"

"Smile. Nobody, Fen, can smile so unsympathetically as the gods."[2]

The novel thus demonstrates how terrible a relationship can be if both persons can again and again be Pygmalion and experience his creative bliss.

The Pygmalion myth is active even in people's dreams. For example, a twenty-five-year-old woman had the following dream: "I am supposed to become the pupil of a Mr. Pygmai, or something like that. He lives where the potter's shop used to be."

The name Pygmai is an important element in understanding this dream. The dreamer knew nobody with such a name. She associated the name to the pygmies, the small people of the African bush. *Pygmaios* also means dwarf; *Pygmalion* could also indicate dwarf. Dwarfs are the creative companions of the Great Mother; it is they who bring forth something and shape it, but they are also small and inconspicuous. The mention of the old potter's workshop—a place where somebody used to be creative—could also refer to being creative.

I asked the dreamer to imagine Mr. Pygmai as a worker in a potter's workshop, to envision what he did and made there, and to ponder what she could perhaps learn from him. In her imagination the woman saw that Mr. Pygmai shaped a woman "with a figure I would like to have and who also expressed the essence I would like to have. He shaped the ideal me, expressed bodily, that I could admire." The woman had always been overweight and did not like to touch or look at her body.

Provoked by the dream and the active imagination, she began over the next few months to shape a female body in clay. By continually having to examine the relationship of the proportions, she very gradually gained some relationship of her own body; thus, through her creative work she also shaped her experience of body and gained an entirely new self-confidence and sense of responsibility for her body.

Pygmalion in her—she did not know the myth—and the woman who was creatively given form were a couple that kept her busy for months and that "schooled" her waking ego-consciousness. It was Pygmalion in her who directed things: She could not get away from the idea of giving shape and form, and she modeled in clay almost compulsively until her body consciousness was so alert that she could dare to enter bodily relationships.

The Pygmalion fantasy is by no means only a male fantasy: many women have strong desires for a Pygmalion who will form/shape them. This desire probably reflects the fact that historically, women's autonomy and sense of responsibility to themselves have been so curtailed that many are not capable of other fantasies of relationship.

Another aspect of the Pygmalion myth has to do with who calls Pygmalion forth. A forty-six-year-old man wrote the following to his female analyst: "You can do anything with me, but do something. Model me into a work of art. Something will occur to you. I have tried for so long to make something of myself, without success." When, and in what situations, do we demand of our mates—or even of our therapist—that they be Pygmalion? We do it when we do not want to take (or perhaps have never taken) responsibility for our own lives and would like someone else to assume responsibility. Pygmalion can give shape so completely only when a creature wants to have no will of its own, no fantasy of its own life, no responsibility. To this extent we all periodically run the danger of conjuring up a Pygmalion, even if we then very quickly curse him.

In therapy it is important that therapists recognize the temptation to be Pygmalion and to interpret the analysand's longing for Pygmalion as a longing for Pygmalion in their own souls. After all, this longing corresponds to the possibility of being Pygmalion, even if perhaps only in the very smallest measure.

All the examples of the Pygmalion myth show how creation and destruction are closely connected. The possibility of destruction is explicitly described in Ingeborg Bachmann's unfinished novel, *Der Fall Franza* [*The Case of Franza*]. This unfinished novel is part of a cycle entitled *Todesarten* [*Ways to Die*]. The novel suggests that women in this society cannot easily survive. In Bachmann's novel,[3] Franza is married to the psychiatrist Jordan. By writing notes about her and leaving them out for her to see, Jordan forces Franza to become a very specific "case." Here the theme is not transformation through love but through destruction:

Why did it never occur to me that he dissects everybody until nothing more re-mained, nothing but a medical finding. [H]e could not see a person beyond the limit he had set him. (p. 402).

From then on I frequently found a slip of paper, sometimes with only a few notes. It took me a long time to understand that; it went on so long, at least more than a year, then I understood that I was the one he had in mind. He worked me up, he prepared me, his case. He drove me to being a case. And every scrap of paper that he let me find drove me further. Then one day I no longer knew any longer when it started. Suddenly, during dinner, eating a Wienerschnitzel, eating fruit, an apple, you know, it was like the piece of apple in the fairy tale, I had this piece of apple in my mouth and began to cough, but I knew that I hadn't swallowed the wrong way, by no means, but suddenly I coughed as if it were poisoned, and after that it went further. . . . (p. 405)

What does a man like Jordan find to hate and to thwart in a person? I think that is it! You thwart the other, you cripple him, you wrest his nature from him, then his thoughts, then his feelings, then you kill what instinct remains in him, the re-maining drive for self-preservation, then you give him a kick when he is finished off. No animal does that; the wolf does not kill the opponent he has humiliated; he cannot kill him; you knew that: he is not capable of biting his throat when he offers it. How wise, how beautiful. And humans, with the strongest weapons the strongest predator, they don't have that inhibition. . . . (p. 413)

He took my possessions from me. My laughter, my tenderness, my ability to be happy, my sympathy, my capacity to help, my animal nature, my radiance—every single time they appeared he trampled them till they no longer arose. But why does somebody do that—that's what I can't understand." (p. 413)

But opposite the destructive Pygmalion is the person who lets herself be de-stroyed. Bachmann may be suggesting in this fragment of a novel that Jordan represents an analytical male society, which grants women no room unless they resolutely defend themselves against this destructive behavior.

A relationship in which the Pygmalion fantasy played a great role was expe-rienced by a man who at the time had considerable difficulties with women: "They are too demanding; they are too domineering, they are not at all sweet; they want to be spoiled." These statements can also mean, "I don't feel up to women's demands; I feel inferior; I am afraid of not being loved enough; I am afraid I will only receive love if I spoil women."

This man met a young woman addicted to medications who was close to de-stroying herself. She worked as a waitress, although she had finished some training and had her certification. He rescued her, was also somewhat in love with her, but above all wanted to get her away from the drugs and the alcohol she was using. He began to put her life in order. She was content: Finally some-one was taking control of her life. (But she secretly confessed that she usually preferred somewhat more dashing men.) He took her to stay with him, scru-tinized her use of drugs, tried to help her find out what sort of work might be satisfying, began to "dress" her, and also decided how she should wear her hair. She was initially satisfied with all of this, but later she said that his actions had really put her off. He began to see artistic possibilities in her and persuaded her to take dancing lessons. The more he saw in her—or projected onto her—the more attractive she became to him. In essence he was saying, "I love your future form."

She admired him for his empathy, his patience, his reliability, his neatness; she found him different from all other men. And in the glow of her admiration, he came to life. He saw himself as important; he could also boast that he had better therapeutic success than many "trained" therapists. In his eyes the young woman was almost well.

She really did get well: She fell in love with a dashing, young man and moved far away from her rescuer. Her rescuer could not understand her actions at all and thus felt betrayed and vengeful.

A year later the woman returned and was again dependent; the other man had left her when he realized how difficult she was. He had also not seen the good in her as clearly as her rescuer had. Meanwhile her rescuer's revenge plans had disappeared superficially. He agreed that they should live together again, and she agreed to marriage. He began to monitor her scrupulously and to work out the plans that seemed to him important for her; she stabilized herself and appeared to be quite satisfied.

Gradually she began to assume some responsibility for herself and developed some interests and aspects of her personality that he had not foreseen, but she retained a great degree of dependence on him and gratitude to him. His response to her increasing independence was an extramarital relationship that happened to offer itself. At this point they came to me for consultation. The wife felt that she was being punished for her independence, from which she had previously always shirked; he felt that he was being punished because his wife no longer needed him as Pygmalion.

This case history makes clear that even a Pygmalion fantasy can have a positive outcome, but that like every fantasy of relationship, it has its appropriate time. Through such a fantasy, something can be brought about that enables a couple to grow into a new form of relationship. In therapy it was pointed out to the husband that his behavior had been so constructive that his wife could now be much more independent, which would take some of the burden off of him. When he realized that an even more interesting relationship was now possible with her, he was able to abandon his attempts to punish her.

The myth of Pygmalion, in which I see both Pygmalion and the woman to be created, is important because this constellation represents a possibility and a danger within all relationships. The Pygmalion myth, like the myth of Shiva and Shakti, is a fantasy of the great love to be attained. But we are not usually conscious of that intention, and neither is our mate, who prefers to be "created" or "educated." This myth also clearly shows how closely related are the life-promoting image of love and the life-inhibiting image of betrayed love.

This myth gave Herbert the opportunity to free himself somewhat from his Shiva-Shakti fascination. It was clear to him that the Shiva-Shakti myth was not to be lived on the level of relationship and that his fundamental problem was his inability to part from another. Thus he began to work out in fantasy the Pygmalion myth, viewing Pygmalion and the woman to be created as aspects of his own soul; but he also learned to perceive the partings of everyday life very consciously and, when it was necessary, to mourn.

Chapter 4

ISHTAR
AND
TAMMUZ

The Goddess of Love and
Her Youthful Lover

I'll be gentle, to you and to me,
We have to be gentle,
with gentle hearts and gentle hands
holding and taking, holding and letting go.
                              —Hugo von Hofmannsthal

Springtime and Death

A forty-five-year-old woman who was accustomed to being courted by men of her age and who was also in amorous relationships with them fell in love with a nineteen-year-old. For him she was the first woman; she introduced him to love, philosophized with him about life, gave him the feeling that he was something like "a young god." For her he embodied the urgent vitality of youth, an "awakening" in the widest sense, and she was happy to bind herself to the young man and his serious love. She did not think that she could also fetter him; from the beginning of their relationship, she knew that their love was transitory: It was the love of a spring that could scarcely last beyond the summer, let alone the autumn and the winter.

In this fantasy of relationship she saw herself as the older, magnanimous woman who could give the young man some of the wisdom of love, and she perceived him to be the "young god" who once again activated in her all the love that she could direct toward a lover and a son.

He saw in her a sort of "goddess of love" who spoiled him and allowed him to be a "divine youth." That he also recognized her maternal characteristics did not greatly disturb him. Both were happy in the intensity of their love.

After a time, however, the young man began to live in a world contrary to the one his motherly friend wanted to show him—for example, if she wanted to acquaint him with the beauty of culture, he announced to her his enthusiasm for motorcross. Hence she had the feeling that she was gradually losing him, and he became a stranger in her eyes. The first shadow of sadness fell over the relationship; the woman was torn between "letting go" and "holding him closer."

Neither could overlook the crisis when the young man fell in love with a girl his own age and left the woman. At first she was sad, furious, disappointed, and felt somewhat exploited. But because the young man still retained the values he had experienced in his relationship with her, she could finally rejoice in his new love. Yet she, grown a little older, remained behind. This typical story suggests the separation of a son from his beloved mother, but it is a genuine love story in which sexuality also played an important role.

This fantasy of relationship is also depicted in the Sumerian myth of Ishtar and Tammuz (ca. 2800 B.C.). The myth has been handed down to us in very incomplete form, yet its basic outlines can be traced with some certainty. The myth presents a matriarchal society in which the mother and love-goddess has a central role, as does her opposite, the son-lover, who represents the dynamic force of change.

In the spring when the new grass sprouts, Ishtar celebrates her sacred marriage with the divine shepherd Tammuz, her son-lover: "He is a figure who, in the most diverse, symbolic forms, tends sheep, protects cattle, and battles lions. He is the 'son,' the 'child,' but equally the 'hero,' the 'manly one,' but especially the 'shepherd.'"[1]

Ishtar is one of the earliest mother and fertility goddesses. She is the mother and spouse of Tammuz and is thus the mother and protectress of the Babylonian kings, who are conceptualized as personifications of Tammuz.[2] The time of the sacred marriage is the time of blossoming and growing vegetation. When the great goddess and her son-lover make love, life can begin to flower, and fertility is assured. Tammuz is invested in preserving life and its herds, which represent vitality itself, for as long as possible.

At the time of summer drought, however, Tammuz must descend into the underworld because a female demon has slain him while he was with his herds. (This female demon is often conceived as an aspect of Ishtar herself.) Ishtar is disconsolate over the loss of her beloved, seeks him everywhere, and also descends to the underworld to seek him in the realm of the death goddess. In her endeavor she also dies, but since she has made appropriate arrangements in the upper world, the gods send her the water of life, and she returns. She goes to the land of Sumer and makes it fertile. As long as she remained in the underworld, the land remained barren.

Ishtar leaves Tammuz, the son-lover, in the underworld; until that point he had not quite understood and recognized her sufferings in the underworld. But then he, too, again resurrects (after 160 days), and a new sacred marriage is celebrated.[3] The renewal of life is thereby symbolically guaranteed: Flowering and dying, plenty and drought follow each other inevitably.

The sacred marriage, the journey to the underworld, and the resurrection that culminates in a new sacred marriage are repeated periodically. The sacred marriage was consummated each time in rites between the high priestess of Ishtar and the king as representative of Tammuz. A wedding hymn from Sumer shows the most important aspects of the divine marriage.[4] The following are relevant verses:

In the palace, in the house that gives
directives to the land, the house of the king
of all lands, in E'ilurugu, the 'black-headed
ones,' all the people have erected a high
throne for the 'Mistress of the Palace': the
king, the god, tarries with her there. That
she decide the fate of the lands, that she
light up on the first good day, complete the
divine order on black monday, let one prepare
on new year's day, the day of cult
celebrations, my mistress' bed, let it be

cleaned with branches of . . . cedar, make it
into my mistress' bed, as a gift lay out
ready a [dress] for her.
That she is pleased in her heart by the
[dress], that she enjoy the bed, one bathes my
mistress for the sacred lap, bathe her for the
lap of the king, bathe her for the lap of
Iddindagans, one washes the holy Innana,
sprinkles the flood with fragrant cedar
resin. The king walks proudly, head erect,
to the holy lap,
Ama'usumgalanna [i.e., Dumuzi, represented by
the king]
tastes of her sacred body.
After the mistress has satisfied herself in
the holy lap of the bed, after holy Innana
has satisfied herself in the sacred lap of
the bed, she speaks to him in the bed:
'I am . . . [the hero's Id] dindagan's.[5]

(Innana is the Sumerian predecessor of the Babylonian Ishtar, and Dumuzi is
another name for Tammuz.)

In this myth it is moving that Ishtar does not simply barter away her son-
lover in the underworld; she seems rather to be painfully touched by the death
of Tammuz, even if she has caused it herself, and she herself goes to the underworld, suffers death, and is again brought to life with the water of life. The only
difference between her and Tammuz is that she has the water of life at her
disposal, whereas Tammuz is dependent on her water of life.

As Ranke-Graves has demonstrated, the Great Goddess was identified in the
matriarchy "with the seasonally determined changes in the plant and animal
kingdoms."[6] In spring, she was depicted as a maiden, in summer as a nymph, and
in winter as the old woman who dwells in the underworld. (Ranke-Graves's idea
is developed by Heide Goettner-Abendroth in her book, *Die Goettin und ihr
Heros* [*The Goddess and her Heros*]).

This threefold manifestation of the Great Goddess was in Greek mythology
three goddesses (Selene, Aphrodite, and Hecate). Originally, however, one
goddess was probably intended in all three forms, which represented the various
phases of life. These phases also offered the male hero three different roles in
life: The longed-for beloved who brings great joy; the warrior against death; and
the one who endures a "dead" time, a time of retreat, in order again to become
the longed-for beloved in a new cycle. The hero is dependent on the mother
goddess and is bound up in her rhythms.

There is a strong emphasis in this myth on the rhythmic, commencing with
the tremendous animation expressed in the rite of the sacred marriage and
continuing in the proximity of love and death. Death is understood here as
"feminine": It is not seen as annihilation but as a transition to new life. It is clear
that the goddess of love, who is also the mother goddess, is always related to
her son-lover in love and in mourning. Again and again she must leave him and is
also left by him, but she always participates in his delight and his pain.

This myth is part of the fantasy of the relationship involving an older woman
with a young man. Many women have this fantasy, in which they see themselves

as similar to the mother/love goddess; they feel confirmed in their womanliness, and they see the beloved as a young god who once again brings the springtime of love into their lives, but to whom they, too, can bring the springtime of love. Women having this fantasy are aware, as Ishtar was, of the transitoriness of this sort of love.

If the union of an older woman and a younger man is becoming more acceptable socially, it is not only because they give something to each other but because in such a fantasy of relationship—or in such a lived relationship—the woman becomes very conscious of her womanhood and her worth. It is not by chance that women today are rediscovering the ancient mother goddesses in their splendor and magnificence. If a woman can identify herself with these mother goddesses, who are, after all, also creators of culture, they then lose their Cinderella complex.[7]

Der Rosenkavalier: A Portrayal from Literature

A love relationship between an older woman and a young man is described by Hugo von Hofmannsthal in *Der Rosenkavalier* [*The Rose Cavalier*]. *Der Rosenkavalier* begins in the bedroom of the Marschallin as Octavian, the "rose cavalier," confesses his love and longing:

Octavian
    Look how my hand reaches for your hand,
    wanting to come to you, to embrace you,
    that's what I am: wanting to come to you;
    but the "I" gets lost in the "Thou" . . .
    I am your boy, but if I then
    go blind and deaf—
    where's your boy then?
Marschallin
    You are my boy! You are my sweetheart!
    I love you!

While he continues to conjure the relationship, she, however, stresses its transience:

Octavian
    Seize her, that's what I want, seize her
    so that she will know whom she belongs to—
    to me! For I am hers and she is mine!
Marschallin
    . . . I feel as though
    I have to sense the weakness
    of everything temporal,
    in my heart of hearts
    how we shall hold on to nothing,
    how we can grasp nothing,
    how everything runs through our fingers,
    everything we reach for dissolves,
    everything melts like mist and dream.
Octavian
    My god! The way she says that.
    She only wants to show me

that she isn't clinging to me.
[*His eyes fill with tears.*]

. . . .

Marschallin
Now I must console the boy
that sooner or later he will leave me.
[*She caresses him.*]
Octavian
Sooner or later?
[*violently*]
Who is putting those words in your mouth,
Bichette?
Marschallin
The words offend you!
Octavian [*puts his hands over his ears*]
Marschallin
Time, Quinquin, time
doesn't change anything.
Time is a strange thing:
if you just live day by day, it's nothing at
all.
But then suddenly, you feel nothing but time.
It's around about us, it's also inside us.
It trickles into your face,
in the mirror it trickles,
it flows into my temples.
And between you and me
it flows again, soundlessly, like an
hourglass.
[*very seriously*]
Quinquin, today or tomorrow you will go away,
and give me up for another
[*somewhat hesitantly*]
who is more beautiful and younger than I.
Octavian
Do you want to drive me from you with words
because your hands won't do you that
service?
Marschallin [*calmly*]
The day will come of its own.
Today or tomorrow the day will come,
Octavian.
Octavian
Not today, not tomorrow! I love you.
Not today, not tomorrow!
If such a day has to be, I won't think of it,
such an ugly day!
I don't want to see that day.
I don't want to think of that day.
Why are you torturing yourself and me? . . .

Marschallin
> Today or tomorrow or the day after.
> I don't want to torture you, my darling.
> I'm telling the truth; telling me as much as
> you.
> I'll be gentle, to you and to me,
> We have to be gentle,
> with gentle hearts and gentle hands
> holding and taking, holding and letting go. . . .
> Whoever is not gentle—life punishes them,
> and God does not take pity on them.

Octavian
> Today you talk like a priest.
> Is that supposed to mean that you
> will no longer let me kiss you till your
> breath expires?

The Marschallin summarizes the essential qualities of such a relationship when she says, "We have to be gentle,/ with gentle hearts and gentle hands/ holding and taking, holding and letting go. . . ." Octavian is then selected to deliver to Sophie the Baron's silver rose. Sophie and Octavian fall immediately and profoundly in love. Of course, this causes great complications, which are finally resolved by the Marschallin.

And as a true lover, she also loves his love for the young woman, even when it hurts her:

Marschallin [to herself, then with
> *Octavian and Sophie]*
> I've promised myself I'd love him in the
> proper way:
> that I would love even his love for another!
> Of course I didn't think
> that it would be laid upon me so soon!
> [*sighing*]
> There are so many things in the world
> so that you'd not believe it
> if you'd hear it.
> Only if you've experienced it, then you
> believe it yet don't know how—
> There stands the boy and here stand I,
> and with the other girl there
> he will be as happy as only men
> understand how to be happy. In God's name![8]

Octavian now has eyes only for Sophie. The Marschallin is abandoned and is left with only her memories. Even if Octavian, as in the myth of Ishtar and Tammuz, had entered the underworld, his resurrection would be in the love of a woman his own age, of whom, however, the Marschallin approves.

In *Der Rosenkavalier*, and in the case of the couple presented earlier in this chapter, the mother-son relationship is addressed in addition to the love affair itself. In *Der Rosenkavalier* and in the case study the young "hero" deserts the maternal lover; in the myth of Ishtar and Tammuz, however, it is the mother/love goddess who leaves Tammuz, and she is afterward plagued by regrets. As always in such affairs, it is not clear who did the deserting and who was deserted; it is a process in which both persons take part actively and passively (and, of course, one person always assumes the more active role).

Mothers and Sons

The Ishtar and Tammuz fantasy plays an important role in the relationship of a mother to her sons and in their mutual separation. Women who are determined to set their sons free, who do not want to bind their sons to them for longer than necessary, and who also want to rear their sons with regard for the equality of the sexes sometimes suddenly catch themselves treating their sons with an attentiveness and fascination that is really exercised only with a son-lover. The mother and her son-lover is a model of human relationship that merits attention. The following case demonstrates some of the issues involved in the mother and son-lover relationship.

A forty-six-year-old woman had a sixteen-year-old son who was vigorously pushing his way into life; he wanted to take charge of his life as much as possible and assume responsibility far beyond his years. His mother trusted that he could take charge of his life to a great extent, and although she understood his urge to live, she was still somewhat concerned. In this context she had the following dream: "I am in an earth temple, under the earth. I know that this is the temple of the Great Mother. As I look around, I discover Christoph (my son) rolled up in a fetal position, sleeping in the corner of the temple. I am frightened and think that something could have happened to him; then I find it appropriate that he is in the temple of the Great Mother."

The dreamer felt that she had released her son to the "Great Mother," that is, to mother nature or to the great mother called "Life." The dream filled her with sadness—it was like taking leave of her son, who now existed in a greater context of life—and yet she was struck by the accuracy of the dream: Her son, like a fetus, was supposed to be born into the sphere of the Great Mother. This aspect of her dream corresponds to the separation process: We separate from our personal parents, and their places are taken by the archetypal parents, whom we meet everywhere, including in ourselves, if we do not cling too greatly to the personal parents. The image of the cave in the dream is most appropriate, for here a maturation takes place in the safety of the earth. Christoph will awaken again later. The woman, who was very closely tied to her son, released him in her dream to the Great Mother, and it would not be surprisng if her son initially had a love affair with an older woman.

This dream can also be understood quite differently: We regard the sleeping son in the realm of the Great Mother as a fantasy of relationship. If this dream is interpreted as a fantasy of relationship, then it illustrates the phase when both—the Great Goddess and her hero—are in the underworld in a time of incubation or maturation when something new can arise. Applied to the mother-son relationship, it would mean that they are in a transition phase of which they are unaware but which they will bear with profound calmness.

If this dream is conceptualized as the inner situation of the dreamer, then it suggests that the son-like qualities in the mother, which link her with life, love, creativity, and the urge to live, place her in the realm of the earth goddess, who is also the goddess of death and who lets things resurrect again only at their appointed time. This expansive drive must be allowed to rest. Such a dormant period could correspond to a less active phase in the life of the dreamer, which she perhaps experienced as boring. But if the dream is viewed as a reflection of the Ishtar and Tammuz myth, then this condition can be understood as a normal phase of a rhythmic process that has profound justification, even if the dreamer would prefer at the time to be full of vitality.

In this dream the constellation of Ishtar and Tammuz presents itself as the interplay of the feminine and the masculine in the human soul. In the son-lover is expressed the fascination with things in the process of becoming, with boundary crossings, with energy. But he is most closely associated with the Great Mother; he is loved, cared for, and protected, but he is also subjected to the transformations of nature, which are not always present but are experienced in rhythms. Through the influence of this masculine element, the woman experiences herself as dynamic, as in movement, and as crossing borders but also as strengthened in her femininity; she assumes a strong identity and vitality in her life. She would gladly let this vital feeling be kept alive by a young hero, who could be a young lover or a son. If this constellation is lived in relationship to a son, the mother will not want to let go of her son. In such a case, the mother identifies with the mother/love goddess and does not see that although she is ultimately rooted in this goddess, she can never be herself in this image. When the son inevitably leaves, the mother remains behind and becomes old, for she has lost everything enlivening that he has embodied and has brought into her life.

Ishtar is deserted, like mothers are deserted; they must return again to the underworld. We must continually recognize that the dynamic feeling for life is transitory and that when we project this feeling onto others, it is expressed in unions that also imply separation. Nevertheless—or precisely because of this—these unions are full of intensity. And just as intensively, we must then mourn the farewells that become necessary.

The Maternal Beloved and the Son

The myth of Ishtar and Tammuz not only concerns women; men also have a longing for this union. A twenty-three-year-old man had the following dream: "I am fishing in a lake. My son—much older than he now is—is very busy, that is, I am constantly afraid that he will invent something crazy. He is just about to rig up a submarine out of a turtle shell. There is a lot of restlessness in the dream. Suddenly I see him talking with a very pretty woman about forty, who radiates calmness. I am satisfied."

In discussing this dream, the dreamer noted first that upon waking, he had hoped his son would at some point be fascinated by an attractive, motherly woman; then his son would no longer be endangered. Only then did it occur to him that the son in his dream was much older than he really was and that the image of his son must also have to do with something son-like in himself that, unprotected, constantly wanted to "invent" something in the world.

This man really did have a difficult time protecting himself. He often hurt himself and frequently did not know when he was tired. He had many good ideas but always tried to realize at least four of them at the same time, and in the end he seldom realized one. He was often very stimulated and had a stimulating effect on others, but instead of feeling good because of this characteristic, he felt driven.

His dream announces that his boyish side, which is so creative and vital, must be united with a maternal lover; perhaps he would then learn to comprehend the creative rhythms of life. Conversely, perhaps the dreamer can try to learn to feel himself into the natural rhythms and to derive the sense of protected vitality, as well as the feeling of calmness, which had radiated from the woman in his dream.

The Relationship of Two Women

Every pole of a fantasy of relationship can be experienced in relation to a man or a woman. This is obvious, for example, when a husband is said to be a mother to his wife, and his wife seeks and finds the mother in him. The fantasy of such a woman would be that each person in the relationship is a father and mother to the other; she could then give her husband something paternal. In a different situation she might seek in him more paternal elements and, by doing so, probably irritate him because until now that aspect of his personality had not been desired; similarly, he could seek more maternal elements in her and equally irritate her. These fantasies occur in a broad spectrum of relationships, including those between people of the same sex.

The fantasy of relationship expressed in the Ishtar-Tammuz myth may be significant in a same-sex relationship, as shown in the following case. Two women—Eva, forty, and Nella, thirty—shared a love relationship. Eva was a potter, looked rather maternal, and was indeed a maternal sort; Nella was a journalist. Between these two women the Ishtar-Tammuz fantasy was very active. Their ideal was a relationship that would bring as much intensity to life as possible, and they hoped that their creative work would be made fruitful by it. Each of them had the feeling that the other could give her that ounce of vitality she needed to be really creative. For both of them, the fantasy of the "sacred marriage" between them was operative. Nella felt that Eva gave her the grounding and security she required in order to shape her "crazy" ideas; Eva, on the other hand, felt that Nella or her love for Nella could give her the dynamism or energy necessary to help her when she sank into an earthy heaviness. Both knew periods when they were not creative and hoped that the other had the water of life at hand. In this fantasy it is clear that each thinks she can be "Tammuz-like" but also "Ishtar-like."

In the actual relationship, Eva increasingly became the caring, motherly lover who enabled Nella to identify with Nella's young, masculine, expansive, dynamic side; Nella's creative unrest continually brought new impulses into the relationship. As their roles got firmer, it was taken for granted that the mate had to fulfill a part of the fantasy; unnoticed, a bit of the autonomy present at the beginning of the relationship got lost. This process, however, occurred only within their own relationship; each could continue to assume either role vis-à-vis other persons, and each could sense both poles of the fantasy as viable possibilities within themselves.

In Eva's life a change began to take place. Once again she completed a course of training and entered a new creative field, and although she had many doubts, she also had a new sense of dynamism and creative joy. It was a period of up-heaval for her, and she was suddenly no longer the embodiment of the caring, loving mother; instead, she experienced a dynamic, energetic, limit-challenging impulse that made her restless and in search of something that would again give her grounding. She sought this grounding from Nella. During this time Nella had experienced no changes, and she did not understand why Eva no longer gave her the mothering that she needed. As always when fantasies of relationship change, a crisis develops in the relationship, as I will show in the next chapter. This crisis forced Eva and Nella to realize that they had concentrated on only one aspect of the fantasy, and Nella became conscious that she had to assume more of a maternal role in their relationship.

Chapter 5

ZEUS
AND
HERA

Couples in Conflict

In a time
in which values have become so uncertain
victory is at least a clear value.

—Client

Z eus and Hera are representative of couples who have celebrated a sacred marriage in which earth is symbolically wedded to heaven and heaven to earth.

A couple, both about forty, entered therapy. I asked them to introduce themselves to me in ways that would characterize their interpersonal relations:

> *He.* I am convinced that I am always right. If I am ever wrong, which doesn't happen very often, usually nobody notices it.
> *She* [*interrupting him*]. No, nobody tells you because nobody can stand the scenes you make when you're petty.
> *He* [*interrupting her*]. I am not petty but you belong to a petty sex.
> *She* [*like a shot from a pistol*]. You stole that sentence from somewhere.
> *He.* You've got to be able to do that, too.
> *She.* I can do that too, but I'm more discriminating about it.
> *He* [*punitively*]. You still haven't introduced yourself right.

He was certainly wrong, for both had introduced themselves impressively in this argumentative exchange, which was rendered at breakneck speed and suggested long practice.

Both these people were trying to dominate the other. Each was invested in determining how to win in every situation and how to avoid becoming the loser. They were not concerned with listening to their mate; instead, their mate gave the cues for a sortie, and every sortie was intended to deal the mortal blow to the other side.

Problems obviously cannot be solved this way. Initially it was not a question of problems at all but rather their insistence that one must never lose. Their struggle is one of principle, and the problem-solving behavior of this couple is rigid, undynamic, and stubborn.

This marriage is one of conflict involving continual mutual humiliation and subsequent revenge; it is, according to Willi, a "symmetrical collusion"[1] or viewed symbolically and mythologically, a Zeus-Hera fantasy of relationship. In this fantasy each member of the couple must prove that he or she is the more powerful, knows better tricks to block or humiliate the other, or is faster at devaluing the other. This form of relationship is quite common and is seen as being rather resistant to therapy. In treating such couples, therapists must be extraordinarily vigilant that they do not get caught in the same pattern of behavior.[2]

A passage from Albee's drama *Who's Afraid of Virginia Woolf?* illustrates some of the dynamics in such relationships:

Martha [*after a moment's consideration*]. You make me puke!
George. What?
Martha. Uh . . . you make me puke!
George [*thinks about it . . . then . . .*]. That wasn't a very nice thing to say, Martha.
Martha. That wasn't *what*?
George. . . . a very nice thing to say.
Martha. I like your anger. I think that's what I like about you most . . . your anger.
  You're such a . . . such a simp! You don't even have the . . . the what? . . .
George. . . . guts? . . .
Martha. PHRASEMAKER! [*Pause . . . then they both laugh*] Hey, put some more ice
  in my drink, will you? You never put any ice in my drink. Why is that, huh?
George [*takes her drink*]. I always put ice in your drink. You eat it, that's all. It's that
  habit you have . . . chewing your ice cubes . . . like a cocker spaniel. You'll
  crack your big teeth.
Martha. THEY'RE MY BIG TEETH!
George. Some of them . . . some of them.
Martha. I've got more teeth than you've got.
George. Two more.
Martha. Well, two more's a lot more.
George. I suppose it is. I suppose it's pretty remarkable . . . considering how old
  you are.
Martha. YOU CUT THAT OUT! [*pause*] You're not so young yourself.
George. [*With boyish pleasure . . . a chant*]. I'm six years younger than you are. . . . I
  have been and I always will be.
Martha [*glumly*]. Well . . . you're going bald.
George. So are you. [*pause . . . they both laugh*][3]

Olympian Marital Conflict

Hera is known as the goddess of marriage and as the jealous, vengeful, sub-jugated spouse of Zeus. Zeus, on the other hand, is regarded as the powerful father of the gods, the highest of all the gods, whom all must obey; he roams freely, and no one—man or woman—is safe from him or his insatiable love. Hence it is sometimes said that Hera's jealousy is because of Zeus' constant cheating. In this simplified and somewhat falsified image, they have become the model for many marriages: she, the crabby wife at the stove, jealous and ill-tempered; he, the roving man of power.

In the *Iliad*, Zeus and Hera's relationship is presented as a constant, Olympian marital battle; indeed, the entire *Iliad*, which depicts the war between the Tro-jans, supported by Zeus, and the Achaians, supported by Hera, seems to me to be a manifestation of their conflict and battle for power. On the following pages, scenes from *Iliad* depict the married life of Zeus and Hera (references are to book and line numbers).[4]

Thetis, the mother of Achilleus, comes to Zeus and implores him as the father of the gods to strengthen the Trojans with the power of victory until the Achaians, whose hero Achilleus was, have sufficiently honored her son. Zeus acts indignant at her demand, and says that Hera troubles him "with recriminations"[5] in the circle of the gods and accuses him of aiding the Trojans. He advises Thetis to go away before Hera notices that she has been there, and he tells her that he will take care of the matter.

But Hera had already noticed that Zeus had taken counsel with Thetis. In the following passage Hera reproaches Zeus on a number of points:

> "Always it is dear to your heart in my absence to think of
> secret things and decide upon them. Never have you patience
> frankly to speak forth to me the thing that you purpose.,"
>   Then to her the father of gods and men made answer:
> "Hera, do not go on hoping that you will hear all my
> thoughts, since these will be too hard for you, though you
>   are my wife.
> Any thought that it is right for you to listen to, no one
> neither man nor any immortal shall hear it before you.
> But anything that apart from the rest of the gods I wish to
> plan, do not always question each detail nor probe me."
>   (I,541–550)

Enraged, Hera counters:

> "Majesty, son of Kronos, what sort of thing have you spoken?
> Truly too much in time past I have not questioned nor probed
>   you,
> but you are entirely free to think out whatever pleases
>   you."
>   (I,552–554)

Nevertheless she then tells him that she is concerned that Thetis may have talked him into something. Zeus cries out:

> "Dear lady, I never escape you, you are always full of
>   suspicion.
> Yet thus can you accomplish nothing surely, but be more
> distant from my heart than ever, and it will be the worse
>   for you.
> . . . ."
> But go then, sit down in silence, and do as I tell you . . ."
>   (I,561–563,565)

Now Hephaistos, Hera's son, enters the marital argument, which could just as easily be taking place between mortals:

> "This will be a disastrous matter and not endurable
> if you two are to quarrel thus for the sake of mortals
> and bring brawling among the gods. There will be no
>   pleasure
> in the stately feast at all, since vile things will be
>   uppermost.
> And I entreat my mother, though she herself understands it,
> to be ingratiating toward our father Zeus, that no longer
> our father may scold her and break up the quiet of our
>   feasting."
>   (I,573–579)

The son attempts to bring his battling parents to their senses, as so often happens in conflictual marriages among mortals. But Zeus misses no opportunity to anger Hera. Once again they are sitting on Olympus and looking down on Troy. "Presently the son of Kronos was minded to anger/Hera, if he could, with words offensive, speaking cross to her . . ." (IV,5–6). In the Olympian view, behind each hero there stood a god who aided him in battle. Zeus thus maintains vis-à-vis Hera and Athene that although they had stood behind Menelaos, it was the pugnacious hero himself, not they, who were victorious. Hera and Athene are offended and ponder evil things for the Trojans because Zeus now wants to give them a victory. Hera is very angry but does not want to have worked in vain for the destruction of the Trojans. Both Zeus and Hera admittedly delighted in destroying each other's cities, and Hera finally says accordingly: " 'Do it then; but not all the rest of us gods will approve you'" (IV,29). " 'Yet my labour also should not be let go unaccomplished; I am likewise a god, and my race is even what yours is'" (IV,57–58). Hera is once again the loser in the rivalry with Zeus, but she reminds him that she, too, is a god and has her dignity.

In general she acts rather resigned: On Olympus she appears alone, and the gods present ask her what is bothering her. All suspect that Zeus has again done something to her. But Hera addresses those present:

"Fools, we who try to work against Zeus, thoughtlessly.
Still we are thinking in our anger to go near, and stop him
by argument or force. He sits apart and cares nothing
nor thinks of us, and says that among the other immortals
he is pre-eminently the greatest in power and strength."
(XV,104–108)

Hera, however, is not always so resigned; sometimes she also employs cunning, if not to be victorious over Zeus, at least to cause him significant problems. When Hera looks down from Olympus and sees that Zeus is again helping the Trojans, she decides to seduce Zeus. She rubs herself with ointments, puts on jewelry, and when she believes she looks attractive enough, she goes to Aphrodite, Zeus' daughter, with a request: "Give me loveliness and desirability" (XIV,198). Thus she intends to go visit her parents, Okeanos and Thethys: " 'I shall go to visit these, and resolve their division of discord,/since now for a long time they have stayed apart from each other/and from the bed of love, since rancour has entered their feelings" (XIV,205–207).

From her bosom, Aphrodite loosens the girdle of love, which works irresistible love in gods and men. Hera now hurries to Sleep and asks him to make Zeus drowsy after she embraces him. Sleep is afraid of Zeus, the thunderer, and remembers how severely they had once been punished by Zeus when they bound him because they could no longer support his arrogance. Yet when Hera promises him one of the younger Graces, Sleep is ready to do what she demands of him. Hera now climbs Mount Ida, where Sleep has already taken his place on a pine tree. Zeus catches sight of Hera at the pinnacle of the mountain, and suddenly a great yearning for her possesses him; this yearning is comparable only to the longing at their first meeting, which they had concealed from their parents. Yet Hera discourages him by saying that she is on the way to her parents in order to bring about their reunion. But Zeus continues to court her and says: " 'Hera, there will be a time afterwards when you can go there/as well. But now let us go to bed and turn to lovemaking'" (XIV,313–314). Zeus embraces his spouse, and at that moment the green grass sprouts beneath them. "So the father slept unshaken on the peak of Gargaron/with his wife in his arms, when sleep and passion had stilled him;/but gently Sleep went on the run to the ships of the Achaians/with a message to tell him who circles the earth and shakes it, Poseidon [that he could now bring help to the Trojans]" (XIV,352–355).

What is here described as Hera's treachery—and whoever needs treachery is always the less powerful—can also be described as the sacred marriage, which guarantees the fertility of the earth. Zeus becomes furious when he sees that he has been tricked, and he reminds Hera of the time he had suspended her from the sky with an anvil on each foot and a golden band about her hands; he had hurled away everyone who had wanted to help her.

No further evidence is necessary to show that there existed between Zeus and Hera a relationship dominated by power (expressed through force and cunning), rivalry, retaliation, and revenge. Why do they have that sort of relationship? Hera seems to feel unheard, misunderstood, and in need of reminding Zeus that she is a goddess. It is important to keep in mind that there are a Cretan Hera and a Cretan Zeus, and an Olympian Hera and an Olympian Zeus. What we have considered so far is the version of the Zeus-Hera myth at the time of the Olympian Zeus, when Zeus was regarded as the father of the gods and men and as the weather god who carried lightning as a weapon and used it as an expression of his power. In contrast, in pre-Olympian, Minoan Crete, where a matriarchal social order dominated,[6] Zeus was a mortal god who was born anew each year of Rhea (a variant of the earth mother Gaia) in Diktaian cave as Hera's brother and was hidden from his father, Kronos, who swallowed his children. In a marriage account from that time, Hera seduces Zeus—as she did later on Olympus—into the sacred marriage according to the model of the mother/love goddess and her son-lover.

In Cretan times, Hera was not the pale, jealous goddess she was on Olympus. (The Olympian version of Hera obviously does not generate much enthusiasm among women.) The Cretan Hera was a great earth mother who appeared in three aspects: as goddess of the mountains and wild animals, comparable to the Olympian Artemis; as nymph goddess who celebrated the sacred marriage with the cretan Zeus on Mount Ida; and as death goddess to whom the oracles were also subject and who was associated with the Python serpent, which symbolized the protection-giving and healing spirit of underworldly powers. (In Olympian times it was said that Hera had given birth to Python in revenge for Zeus' having given birth to Athene from his head.) In Minoan Crete, which was destroyed about 1400 B.C. by a volcanic eruption, Hera was regarded as goddess of agriculture, weaving, cooking, and medicine. She was the ruling goddess of pre-Hellenic Greece.[7]

Another Cretan marriage account depicts Zeus' subordination to Hera. If Zeus really wanted to attain rulership over the gods, he had to subordinate himself. When Zeus had vanquished his father, Kronos, he courted Hera. After she rejected him, he approached her as a disheveled cuckoo, and also let a rainbow descend; Hera took the cuckoo sympathetically to her bosom to warm it. Then Zeus, the cuckoo, again changed back into Zeus, father of the gods, and wanted to ravish her. She yielded on the condition that he marry her: "Hera's forced marriage with Zeus symbolized the conquest of Crete and of the Mycenaean, i.e., cretanized, Greece, and the fall of its hegemony in both lands."[8]

With that, however, the transition from the pre-Olympian matriarchy to the patriarchy of Olympian times was accomplished. Zeus takes the double axe, which on Crete had still belonged to Hera. Now their subsequent conflicts become more understandable: Hera had truly forfeited much of her significance and wanted to restore it and the *Weltanschauung* she had embodied; Zeus, on the contrary, must assert his dominance at all costs. His assertion of dominance is also shown in his assumption of all the capacities that had been ascribed to the mother goddess and that had characterized her. Thus he bears children—from his head and from his thigh. In the conflict between the matriarchy's aftereffects and the arising patriarchy may lie the deeper reason for the perpetual battle between Zeus and Hera. In this conflict Hera had been so devalued that she had to avenge herself. The assertion that Hera was obnoxious because of her jealousy —as writers continually try to persuade us—is scarcely tenable: In myth, Hera is primarily regarded as the spouse of Zeus and is not there to be mother of his children; for that he has other consorts. Zeus' infidelity as the sole motive for her jealousy is minimally insightful. Also, Hera herself can have children, independently of Zeus. We could thus understand the conflict between Zeus and Hera as the problems associated with transition, which last until a new union has been achieved. Meanwhile, the model of Zeus and Hera has been an enduring one. Greek mythology could really be a matter of indifference to us if it had not so greatly influenced our thinking, especially in the form of the later mythology of the Olympian period.

We experience conflicts like those of Zeus and Hera in our psyche and also in our everyday life—for example, when an old and a new current are equally strong, or when the new must win but the old will not disappear or perhaps must be just as strong so that the new can contrast itself to it. However, such situations, which produce powerful tensions, are transitional.

Developmental Possibilities of a Conflictual Couple

Strangely, Zeus and Hera always stay together, although there can really be no talk of love between them. Conflictual couples usually also stay together. The couple whose "introductory conversation" I sketched earlier in this chapter came into therapy because they could not leave each other but found life together very difficult. Moreover, their children were growing up and beginning to fight exactly as they had seen their parents fight, and the parents found that unbearable. Conversely, their children found their parents' fighting unbearable. Just as Hephaistos had admonished Zeus and Hera, these children implored their parents to be reasonable. The couple also had sexual problems: He often experienced premature ejaculation and she was sometimes anorgasmic. In the context of the conflictual marriage, these sexual problems can be viewed as mutual punishment. Because they had an agreement to tell each other everything, they sometimes had to talk for hours about how they could live in a relationship outside of the marriage. Then every possible partner of the other was immediately devalued. Both reacted with tremendous jealousy but neither was able to empathize with the other if he or she showed jealousy. The control they exerted over each other was enormous.

At the beginning of one therapeutic session, only the husband was present because the wife had been delayed by traffic. Although I was aware of the potential hazards involved in holding a session with only one of them, I was curious to see how this man would behave if he were there without his wife. I started the session with him alone until his wife arrived (who, by the way, did not object). He had always produced a somewhat "inflated" effect when he was with his wife—he had always somehow put on airs—yet when alone he had a rather depressive, "caved-in" effect. He complained that his wife could enter into relationships with other people much more easily than he, and he even suspected she had love relationships. Although they did have an agreement to tell each other everything, he did not really believe that she did. Admittedly he always had a bad conscience whenever he wanted to enter a relationship, but if his wife had a relationship, he had to have one too. Sadly overtaxed, he said that he could not possibly lag behind his wife. He also recognized how much energy he expended in this contest, but he considered this form of relationship to be his fate.

I asked them both about fantasies of relationship. He replied as follows: "With other women I have beautiful fantasies of what they could do with me and I with them; with my wife I always have the image of what she could stir up to humiliate me. Then if she doesn't look at me when I want her to look at me, I fantasize how I could punish her for that, for example, how I could tell her something in a bored tone of voice."

The wife responded in the following way: "I used to have fantasies; then he seemed to me like a young god. But now I only think: What sort of little game is he hatching now? I fantasize that he could take up an outside relationship with another woman whom I simply couldn't stand and he couldn't either, because basically we have the same tastes. He could really get to me with that, and also by talking about our relationship with people that I don't like. I saw too late that I mustn't show him where he can get to me."

This couples' fantasies of relationship move predominantly in the Zeus-Hera realm. The man talks about having beautiful fantasies involving other women, but he does not elaborate on them. The wife's final comment—that she should never have shown where she was vulnerable—reveals where the tragedy lies in a marriage based on power and control: In this constellation neither of them may be emotionally open; neither may show any weakness because it would only be exploited. They must repress their weaknesses as well as a great many experiences and emotions.

In this relationship, exercise of power and control have taken the place of love; instead of idealizing, they devalue. Yet this couple feels very close to each other, and to the question of a possible separation fantasy both answer that although they constantly talk about it, they do not want a separation.

The couple achieves closeness to each other through conflict and struggles for power. Fighting is their chance of attaining the greatest possible closeness with the greatest possible delineation from each other. Closeness and delineation can be experienced simultaneously. And through conflict they have a sense of overcoming the separateness from each other, even if this form is taxing.

The wife was the first to bring a dream into therapy: "Court. A woman and a man judge are debating with each other. The debate is very interesting and has rules understood by nobody but themselves. In the courtroom there are many babies who are screaming and are probably hungry, but nobody takes note of them. They scream so loudly that you can hardly understand the judges. I look at all this from a gallery and wonder if I should go to the babies. After all, they need somebody."

The wife could not develop this dream much. The court meant nothing to her, but she expressed concern for the babies: They are in the wrong place, she thought, and they really ought to be held and fed.

I offered her the subjective-level interpretation* that these babies represented new possibilities of life in her that must be held and fed. I suggested that perhaps she also sometimes had the need to be held and fed instead of having her relationships always follow the "who is right" (court) model.

This dream also suggests that the two debating judges represent possibilities for experiencing and processing within herself, but the babies have come to the fore through their crying. It also contains some criticism of me, for only the two debaters can understand the rules of the debate. In case I had wanted to or had felt I had to understand in this situation, she would have hit me. I did not share these ideas with her; I only took up the element concerning the babies.

In reply to my interpretation her eyes lit up a little, and she said that she sometimes would like to be treated like a baby, but if her husband did not want to treat her this way, then she could not give in to such "female demands." Although the dream pointed to a possible opening, the situation remained as it had been—blocked.

There are various reasons why a couple would relate so much on this level of power. First I must add that this couple did not play Zeus and Hera from the beginning; both initially described themselves as an extraordinarily loving couple for whom there had hardly ever been any differences, since both of them had always wanted the same thing and had loved each other so much.

In the description of their courtship they revealed that they had both had a very romantic fantasy of relationship at that time. They had simply tuned out conflicts and were obviously very symbiotic. As long as they were not living together, they could maintain boundaries and also allow room for intimacy, since they had to experience it only temporarily. Their difficulties began after the wedding, when they shared an apartment for the first time.

One explanation for the rivalrous power collusion is that these people are seeking and can find the greatest possible closeness with the greatest possible differentiation at the same time. An examination of each person's family background can extend this explanation and also cast a light on how such a Zeus-Hera constellation can come about and manifest intrapsychically.

Both came from families in which the women were strong and in the majority. In the wife's family there already was a Zeus-Hera constellation in her parents; she had a strong mother who continually rivaled her father, who also acted strong. They always criticized each other, but as soon as someone else criticized either of them, they pulled together. The children learned that if they attacked their parents, their parents acted as if they lived in harmony. The wife had thus learned the Zeus-Hera behavior from her parents. She liked the fact that her mother was

---

*In Jungian dream interpretation, "a figure is characterized as *objective* when it appears in the dream as an actual person in his actual relationship with the dreamer. The figure is characterized as *subjective* when it appears in the dream as portraying part of the dreamer's personality." (Mattoon, *Applied Dream Analysis: A Jungian Approach* [Washington, D.C.: V. H. Winston & Sons, 1978], pp. 111ff.)—TRANS.

a strong woman who did not always submit to her husband, but she also thought her mother was not feminine enough. She sensed that she herself was also a strong woman, but she also demanded of herself that she be a "proper" woman without denying her strength. "Proper" meant being all those things that make up the current female stereotype, and for her these included compliancy, softness, impressionability, and so on. These wishes and vital possibilities were in conflict with her strength, which she initially regarded as only "masculine."

The husband came from a family in which his mother and grandmother were responsible for earning the money so that his father, an unsuccessful artist, could dedicate himself to his art. The man felt that the two women and his sisters had been pleasant and that his mother in particular had been solicitous and warm-hearted; but he demanded of himself that he now be a "real" man.

Both persons in this couple had strong "feminine" as well as "masculine" components. If the man and woman had not demanded of themselves that they thoroughly conform to their respective gender stereotype, they probably could have had a rich relationship from the beginning. The woman was more conflicted about herself than he; after all, she had to be "feminine" and also very strong. She was thus very much divided in herself and made her husband responsible for her own inability to express her needs for tenderness. When the feminine and the "masculine" components are equally strong in a person, but for some reason only the "feminine" or only the "masculine" may be lived, the other components create an intrapsychic conflict resulting in aggression, devaluation, and dominance.

The conflict phase would have been a transitional one if they had seen through their game and if each had consciously recognized how great his or her "feminine" or "masculine" needs were. The conflict phase could have been a fruitful period because they might have come to know themselves far better in connection with each other. This would have been a transitional phase if each person's domineering behavior had not been so vital to each: He believed that a "real" man had to be in charge at all times; she was not willing to play a subordinate role, which, in terms of her psychic structure, was unsuitable. Since both of them had the same fundamental problem—namely, an inability to reveal their "feminine," yielding side—and each perceived the other as domineering, their relationship stabilized around their conflicts.

We were marking time, so I asked both of them to conjure up the fantasy of a good marriage. He said the following: "I see myself with a young, soft, cuddly woman lying in a spring meadow; she gives me something good to eat; I also can spoil her. We simply enjoy and love each other. I see myself as an older, sovereign man who stands above things, makes the decisions, and gets admired for it."

The woman had this fantasy: "I am climbing a mountain with a young, interesting man. Along the way we sit down under a rock ledge because there is a thunder shower. We love each other and are happy that we are not alone. I would like to be completely devoted to someone and not always have to defend myself."

These images of a good marriage expressed new fantasies of relationship, which could be accompanied by change. He sought to realize the model of the older man and the young girl, a model familiar to us from tales of Zeus and the nymphs. This is the father-daughter model, known to us also from accounts of Simon Magus and Helen, Merlin and Viviane, Faust and Helen, as well as Hatem and Suleika in Goethe's *West-Eastern Divan*. It is a fantasy of relationship in which the old man sees himself as the one who, in love, gives his entire experience of life—and, in the case of Zeus, his entire power—to a woman; in return, he receives her youth, admiration, and vitality. As a fantasy involving a mate, however, it is the father-daughter relationship and the renewal associated with it that are involved here.

To the man, the father-daughter constellation offered the possibility of youth and of outwitting death, because through the new mate he realized again that he was no longer young. This constellation also implied that the older man would be the dominant one because he had more experience with life. In the daughter's role, a woman's autonomy is diminished. This model of relationship also offered the man power, which he could retain while loving. This model seemed to suggest a way out of the couple's dilemma, but at first it existed in fantasy; a transition had not yet been effected.

The wife's fantasy of relationship showed that she too, was looking for a way out: She saw herself with an interesting young man. To the question of how she saw herself in this fantasy, she said, "Maternal, but very pretty and very seductive; in any case, I set the tone; I say what we're going to do." Her fantasy corresponded to the model of the Great Goddess and her son-lover—that is, to the Ishtar-Tammuz model. The mother-son model derived from an earlier historical period of matriarchy is active in the woman.

The woman's fantasy of relationship was somewhat more exciting than her husband's fantasy. She wanted to climb a mountain, that is, to exert herself and also to have an overview from an elevated standpoint. But there is also a thunderstorm in her fantasy, suggesting that the cave can be experienced as very protective and sheltering, even in an electric storm. Moreover, the rocky ledge in her fantasy could be the cave in Crete where the young god Zeus is reborn. To this extent matriarchal structures were visible.

Regardless of this fantasy, they continued to fight like Zeus and Hera, humiliating each other and attempting to be the victor over the other. Then he uttered the following: "In a time in which values have become so uncertain, victory is at least a clear value." I attempted to get them to listen to each other; I trained them to exchange "I messages," to tell each other their feelings and not only make reproaches and list the other's deficiences; I encouraged them to work out fantasies of relationship. For a long time very little happened.

To give the reader some sense of the length of this unfruitful phase, I will leave this conflictual couple for a while before discussing the solution to their problems. In the next chapter I will focus on the familiar model of the older man and the young woman, which is a common fantasy of relationship.

Chapter 6

MERLIN AND VIVIANE

The Wise Old Man and the Young Girl

> *Hatem.*   *You make blush, like red of morning,*
> *This high summit's dour retreat,*
> *And once more there comes to Hatem*
> *Breath of spring and summer's heat.*
>
> *Suleika.*   *Love shall give to love its power,*
> *I shall lose you nevermore!*
> *To my youth you bring the flower*
> *Of your passion strong and pure.*
>
> Goethe

Merlin's Enchantment in the Whitethorn Hedge

Merlin and Viviane, described in medieval epic, represent the model of the older man and the young girl. There is something special about this couple: At the end of their tale, Viviane is free and Merlin is enchanted. Their situation is in contrast to that of Zeus, for example, who simply abandons his nymphs to their fate after every liaison. Viviane's freedom is an important aspect of the older man/young girl model, because it suggests that although the young woman may be diminished in such a relationship, she can also become more autonomous because of it.

There is something else that is special about this story: Today we are experiencing something like a Merlin renaissance in the republication of books about Merlin and in films and dramas about him.[1] If Merlin is reappearing in our collective fantasy, then surely that means something "Merlinian" is lacking. Merlin withdrew from the world through his relationship to Viviane. Perhaps consideration of the story of those two will give us ways in which a new Merlin—not simply another form of the old Merlin—could come alive for us today.

In *Merlin oder in das Wuste Land* Tankred Dorst tells the story, of Merlin and Viviane:

In the forest of Broceliande the ancient Merlin, dropped out of time, meets the maiden Niniane [Viviane]. With a twig he describes a magic circle about himself and his beloved. Music resounds, they see dancing maidens. The flowers and grasses become more fragrant. The sun rises higher in the sky. A hedge has grown up and shelters the lovers from the curious eyes of the world. The magic of play, the magic of love. Amorous play. Ninane asks her ancient lover to reveal to her the spell that produces such magic. Merlin, filled with the anticipation of her surrender, grants her request. It is an exchange, but not a bargain. He gains her youth, she the wisdom of his age. After they have slept together, Merlin lays his head in the lap of his beloved. His fingertips trace the contours of her cheeks, her lips, her breasts. Reality and dream blur. Then she arises, murmurs the magic word nine times. Now the magic is irreversible. Again she sits down, beds the dreamer's head on her lap. Merlin awakes. It seems to him as though he lies on a bed in a high tower. Then he comprehends what has happened. He says to Niniane, "You will have betrayed me now if you do not always remain with me, for nobody but you can take me out of this tower." "My dear beloved," she answers, "I will often lie in your arms." And the girl keeps her promise. Only a few days and nights pass when she is not with him. Merlin cannot budge from the spot. But she comes and goes as it pleases her.[2]

In the Middle Ages the whitethorn was regarded as a symbol of caution (the caution one needed to pluck a whitethorn) but also of hope.[3] We will cautiously approach the whitehorn bush, wishing all the while that we do not lose hope.

Robert de Boron[4] relates the story of Merlin and Viviane more expansively and colorfully; I will draw on his account in order to increase our understanding of this couple.

According to de Boron, Viviane is the daughter of a vassal named Dyonas whose dwelling was often visited by the goddess of the forest, Diana. It was Diana who had promised Dyonas, her godson, that his first child would be a daughter, and after Diana's death, this daughter was supposed to be so greatly desired by the wisest man in the world that she "would come into great authority at the time of Uther Pendragon." And so it came to pass, as Diana had said: Dyonas sired a daughter who was given the name Viviane.

In de Boron's account, Merlin and the very young Viviane meet at a spring "that spreads out forming a beautiful, clear pond." Viviane often played here. At their first meeting, Merlin assumed the form of a handsome nobleman. He told her that he "could make a castle rise up on the spot," that he could walk on water without getting his feet wet, and make a river flow where previously none had been. Viviane also wanted to learn these tricks; in return she offers to be his confidante and beloved all the days of her life. Merlin is delighted by this; Viviane is cautious. Merlin makes magic, but she wants to learn to make magic before she gives him a "pledge of her love." After she learns from him that he can foresee the future, she is satisfied that she could benefit from such arts.

Once again Merlin leaves Viviane. He goes to his old teacher, Blasius, and takes leave from King Arthur. He says to Blasius that this will be his last visit because now he is going to Viviane and has no more power to depart from her or to come and go according to his own will: "I am so spellbound by her love."

He goes to Viviane, and she continually has him teach her his arts. He teaches her so many of them that "for all times he was regarded as a magician. He still has this reputation. She retained in her memory everything she learned and wrote it down."

Viviane ponders what she could still learn from him. Her need is to bind him to her for all time and eternity. "Please, teach me how to enclose a man by magic power without a tower and without a wall and without iron so that he never again can escape except I will it. When Merlin heard these words, he hung his head and began to sigh from the depths of his heart." He confesses to her that he is so bound by her love that he must execute her will. But Viviane declares to him that her great love for him completely fills her, and her every thought and desire is for him. "Since I love you and you love me, is it not then right that you do my will and I yours?" Now Merlin is joyously convinced and asks Viviane her will. "Lord, I will that you teach me to create a beautiful and lovely place which I can seclude so completely with my art that it can never be broken open. Let us be together there, you and I, as often as pleases us, in joy and bliss." Merlin wants to conjure this place for her. But she says, "Lord, I do not at all want that *you* create it, but that you teach me how *I* can make it, for I want to make it as best suits my will." This, too, Merlin grants.

One day as they walk through the forest, they find a beautiful whitethorn bush, covered with blossoms. There they sit down, Merlin lays his head in the maiden's lap, she caresses him tenderly, and then he falls asleep. As he is sleeping, Viviane arises, begins to draw a circle around him and about the bush, speaks her magic words, steps again into the bush, and again lays his head in her lap and holds him until he awakes. When he awakes "it seems to him as though he is in the most beautiful tower in the world and is lying on the most beautiful bed." He says to Viviane, "Noble Woman, you will have betrayed me if you do not remain with me; for no one save you has the power to dissolve the spell of this tower." She promises him that she will often be with him, and also keeps her promise. He can never again leave this fortress that Viviane has created for him, but she comes and goes as often as she will.

However we assess Merlin's retreat from the world—and it has been assessed variously (for instance, that he fell under the power of eros and sexuality and thereby sacrificed his magic powers)—he is certainly not dead; he is confined to the forest from which he had come. His knowledge and his power are in the hands of Viviane and hence are not lost, even if initially it is not clear what she will do with them.

Does Merlin intend to suggest with his planned and "foreseen" retreat that he is no longer to be found in the world of external conquests, is no longer concerned with Arthur's wars, is no longer behind the quest for the Grail in the original form but is now to be encountered in "love" and in relationship generally? Does he decide this of his own accord, or is it implied in the sagas that his workings are now of a fundamentally different sort ("the ancient Merlin, dropped out of time . . .")?

We meet Merlin mysteriously concealed in the forest and bound to Viviane, indissolubly. Their love is a half-idyll, half-tragic entanglement. Certainly the battle of the sexes is contained in their tale: The roaming, continually changing Merlin is spellbound by a woman, and now the woman can roam. Hetmann considers this union a metaphor for "the abrogation of the sovereign authority of the one sex over the other."[5] Goettner-Abendroth sees in their union the matriarchal form of relationship in which the woman chooses her beloved and the man subjugates himself to her so that true love then rules.[6]

Merlin and Viviane's union, which binds them simultaneously, takes place in the forest; perhaps it is from this place that we can lure them forth again.

Both Merlin and Viviane belong in the forest realm. Merlin resides in the magic forest, in the "valley of no return."[7] This entire forest borders on the beyond, that is, on the uncanny, which confronts individuals in their search for the path in the darkness of the forest. The forest shelters and conceals life, nourishment, animals, and the secrets of nature; individuals must enter it in order to reveal and expose it all. Thus the forest has become a symbol for those aspects of our soul that we shelter from our everyday life. It is also a place where a wildly voluptuous vegetation dominates, where our animal sides enjoy themselves or tear each other to shreds, where it is somewhat dark—things are not so clearly transparent—and full of life but also somewhat threatening. It is a world of retreat and of things that refresh or frighten us. The retreat often has the character of an initiation in which we must survive, endure, and carry through a transition from one phase of our life to another.

We experience the forest in ourselves when we no longer know what to do and abandon ourselves to our fantasies. When we no longer control our fantasies and are able to immerse ourselves in the images they offer us, when we clearly perceive our emotions and our drives, we are in the forest. We usually call this a state of chaos because we can see no order in it. But emotions and drives do have an order that is appropriate to them, just as the wildly rank forest has an order. If we are in the forest too little, however, we do not understand its order. If we always avoid or split off our emotions and drives as things that should not be, then we will never penetrate their order and will experience them as chaotic and frightening. The fantasies that I associate with the forest are of the color "green"[8] because they have to do with continual renewal and thus with hope. But there is no becoming without a passing away.

Merlin's castle, with its famous "windows without number," is situated in the forest. As master of the wilderness, he has a house with an infinite number of entrances and just as many exists; it invites one to tarry, but it also returns the seeker to the world.

As master of the wilderness, Merlin has a way with fantasy, imagination, images, and imaginings. He is so closely linked to nature that he knows her laws and hence can foresee—not preplan, but preview. Thus he embodies the order concealed in wildly voluptuous nature, and hence he also has a way with plants. Perhaps these plants also play a role in the creation of visions and imaginings; then there would also be an element of the dangerous and uncanny involved.

Can Merlin work magic because he senses greater interconnections? Can he therefore be the counselor of the kings who send knights on the quest for the Grail? Can he create an entire vision of the Grail, a fantasy about what this highest value could be? Can he therefore seduce the knights into seeking this highest value? In the quest for the Grail, the path is the most important aspect, which suggests the need to search for the concealed meaning behind all appearances, behind all living things, behind life and the experiences that one has in life. We do not really know what the Grail really is, even if there are many explanations for it. The Grail represents a highest value, and as such it contains a "surplus of meaning" and beckons us to seek its hidden meaning.

To devalue our fantasies and imaginings is to banish Merlin again to his forest. We have a special ability to create images of all possible aspects of life. Imaginings are neither good nor bad, but whether ideas work out to be good or bad has to do with what we do with them. In fantasy we create our world, our view of the world, our relationships to people, God, and nature. Our perceptions are always mingled with our inner images (even if we believe that we are ever so objective, there is always a bit of imagination linked to our perceptions). At issue here is not avoiding imaginings but rather trusting and refining them so that we understand their laws and their contribution to our grasp of reality. In our imaginings, our conscious world not only reveals itself but our unconscious world as well. In our imaginings we move along the borders and are citizens of two worlds. There we give shape to what makes us anxious, what makes us happy, what moves us; there we give shape and form to ourselves. The images that we have of ourselves have a great influence on our self-understanding. We do not make these images in the imagination; we bring them forth in the imagination.

We all know that dreamy, intuitive vision is less highly regarded today than rigorously logical, clear thought. Naturally the danger in dreams and intuitions is that we will "get lost in the forest": Fantasms can grow out of fantasies, and vision can overflow into visions that carry us out of the human world. But logic also has its pitfalls, and logic is inappropriate when a situation calls for intuition or feeling. Clear thought can mislead us into mistaking a problem for the whole when it is actually only a small segment of a global problem. This often leads to our finding solutions that in the end create more problems than they solve.

According to saga, Merlin played a great role in the life of King Arthur. If he is an archetypal figure, perhaps he also influences us today as the "wise old man" who embodies the wisdom of humanity and the human ability to sense and see in union with nature. Merlin's connection to nature is strongly emphasized. He has the power to interpret life, and through his vision he also gives hope that life can be mastered. We know yet other personifications of the figure of the wise man (Lao-tse, for example), but they belong less to the realm of nature. Merlin, however, is completely bound to the realm of nature. And if I say that he can stand for the effective power of the imaginative, then this imaginative works in him in a distinctly marked form. He is to be seen in the ranks of those shamans who dreamt the great dreams for the clan, who beheld the great images for the community.

We have those shamans no longer. The times are past in which an Arthur "cared for" those subjects entrusted to him; today it is the responsibility of each person to find his old wise man and her old wise woman in the soul. Merlin personifies wisdom, which finds its expression in the human imaginative capacities and in trust in and correspondence to the rhythms of nature. Like Merlin, the person who has these imaginative capacities is a "magician" who can change the world in a magical manner, for through the imagination we change, we charm the world, we charm ourselves.

I think that Merlin is misunderstood if we link him with black magic. The fact that he is enchanted by his own imaginative capacities suggests to me that imagination also forms and shapes us. I view his being enchanted not so much as a misfortune but as a conclusion to his work, as a conscious sacrifice in the sense of *stirb und werde* [die and become] so that he can become active in a new form.

The wise old man or wise old woman is a figure practically every person, consciously or unconsciously, summons in longing. This wish is often projected: We would like to have a relationship with an old person who knows about life and what decisions to make in delicate situations because he or she sees the larger context and has experience. The reason why younger persons are often disappointed has to do with their finding not a wise old man or wise old woman but rather only an old person. Indeed, some old persons do not have wisdom, but the disappointment also stems from projecting the image of the wise old person onto another when it is really necessary to find the wise old person in ourselves. In our imaginations and dreams, we initially long for a figure who knows "where things are going," for a hand that reaches out protectively toward us and leads us, even if we behave autonomously. The longing for the wise old man or woman, however, can also lead to a greater understanding of this figure and thus to our becoming wiser ourselves.

In our dreams wise old persons often appear, usually when there is a difficult situation we have to deal with but in which our own powers do not seem sufficient. The appearance of a wise old man or woman is usually of the greatest significance for the dreamer because a new view of life, and hence also new possibilities in life, opens up. The danger lies in our identifying with this old wise person and thereby overreaching ourselves by behaving as if we were the wise old man or woman. Merlin comes and goes—unexpectedly—and that is how the figures of the wise old person exist in our life; they are not on call.

Merlin is a forest dweller but he is also at home in the world of spirit, as his background would suggest: His mother was a princess or a nun, his father an incubus (a devil). This touches on the issue of heathenism and Christianity. Merlin could be an integrating figure, a symbol that a new spiritual current must always unite with the old current if it is to endure. His living on the edge of the forest could be a hint that in him are united forest and open country, nature and spirit, Christian and heathen, patriarch and matriarch.

Viviane as Learned Nymph

Viviane is one of the learned "fairies" of the Middle Ages. She knows what she wants and is on her guard vis-à-vis Merlin. She owes her possibility of charming Merlin to Diana. According to Zimmer, Diana is a siren and a great sea goddess from Sicily, and Merlin, for his part, likes to play with water.[9] Among the Celts, nymphs are female deities and nature deities who watch over springs and rivers.[10] Springs are places where this world and the other world come in contact; it is where the overflow of the earth's interior collects and flows out upon the earth. We associate springs with images of water that is overflowing and repeatedly gushing forth; the spring is actually an earth womb that gives again and again.

Nymphs must take care that these springs fulfill their function; they are the servants of the Great Mother, for whom these springs are a symbol of birth and overflowing abundance. To this extent Viviane as nymph is there to fulfill Diana's will that something new shall always be coming into the world.

To the Greeks, the nymphs were part of Artemis' retinue; the Romans called this goddess Diana. We, too, are probably dealing with Diana. She is a goddess of the moon and mistress of animals and untamed nature. As such she is also a goddess of vegetation and fertility. The springs, rivers, and swamps are sacred to her, and hence she is again associated with fertility. She is the protectress of nature and is responsible for nature's thriving; she is therefore responsible for everything useful to humankind. She embodies nature, and through her all nature becomes a goddess; humankind must keep the company of nature just as one keeps the company of a goddess.

Merlin is united with the forest and the springs. His appearance in newly transformed shapes suggests that he has features of a water deity, since the essence of water deities is their continually shifting shapes. (For example, in the myth of Proteus, Menelaos wants to learn the future from him; Proteus, the Ancient of the Sea, withdraws by changing himself into various animals.) Springs are associated with the power of prophecy and are thought to be in contact with the other world, and wisdom can be found where the other world touches this world. In looking at a spring we center ourselves, we gaze into ourselves; our inner images can emerge, and we in turn become capable of seeing. If Merlin is so united with forest, nature, and spring, why must he still fall in love with Viviane? Or does Diana perhaps have the intention of uniting this man with Viviane? Is Diana perhaps jealous, since Viviane is supposed to unite with Merlin only when Diana has died? Was Diana previously Merlin's companion?

Is the issue here that women must win back the magical power—the female magical power—that Merlin has? (Prophecy, of course, has been the province of prophetesses since ancient times.) Would Diana like to keep the upper hand? Is it then a question of a struggle between matriarchal and patriarchal currents? Or is something else involved: Through Viviane does Diana want to bind the realm of her efficacy to the realm of Merlin's workings?

Mutual Animation

If Merlin and Viviane already dwell in similar surroundings, informed by similar realms and responsible for them, what can they then give to each other? We must keep in mind that we have before us an old man and a young girl. When a couple is composed of an old man and a young girl or an old woman and a young boy, the renewal of life is a central issue (cf. the sacred marriage of the mother goddess with a young god, such as that of Ishtar and Tammuz celebrated in the spring). This can be confirmed in everyday life: Between very young and very old persons there is frequently an interesting "exchange." The young person rejuvenates the old person and receives from that person a concentrated experience of life, a "preliminary outline" of an entire life.

The union of the ancient Merlin with the young Viviane accordingly suggests that he must present himself in a new way. Viviane brings him her youth and her love, which transmit sensuality and fascination as well as containment and protection. She gives him shelter, which we do not really know whether to praise as the "wonderously beautiful tower" or to lament as a prison. From whichever perspective we view it, we will experience his state of enchantment differently. To a knight of Arthur's, for whom roaming was essential, Merlin's shelter was a prison and a cause for sympathy. Whoever wants to put down no roots finds it foolish to let himself be thus enchanted. To Knight Gawain's question of how Merlin, the wisest of all men, could let himself be thus enchanted, the historians have Merlin reply: "At the same time I am also the most foolish man, for I love another more than myself."[11]

It seems to me as though Merlin had exchanged the world of fame for the world of love, convinced that what is, is that which must be—viewed from a seer's vantage point. That is his place. Perhaps, however, he is only now really united with Diana, the moon goddess, the mother goddess, and thus with the possibility of again being rejuvenated? The new life form in which he appears would be from within; he gives people his special attributes: guide of souls, magician, wise man who nevertheless always has something perplexing, not entirely comprehensible, about himself. The whole thing is arranged by Diana and hence expresses a more matriarchal view of life.

Viviane is the first to awaken in Merlin the longing to be united with her. She remains true to the love that grows between them. But what does Merlin bring to Viviane? He brings her the longing to be able to enchant and to cast spells according to *her* will. "Clairvoyant inspiration is the gift of the nymphs," says Plato in the *Phaedrus*; so to what end does Viviane need Merlin? To be able to make real what she sees, to transpose it into the deed. He loves forth from her the longing to be able to change the world but also to enchant the beloved.

Here we must see not only the "enchanted" Merlin but also a binding union. Nymphs are creatures that do not particularly like to be bound. They have many erotic and sexual adventures at their springs, but they do not like to commit themselves. Thus Viviane, too, is offered a form of life new to her.

But what good to us is the new form of relationship if in it the wise old man is enclosed in a sort of Sleeping-Beauty castle? Or must we understand it otherwise: Is Viviane a new embodiment of nature and spirit, this time in the shape of a woman, and thus represents a female wisdom in which love and committed relationship become visible? Seen this way, Merlin's tower would be a symbol of a womb, a place of transformation: from no commitment, from the joy in the sudden fancy, from roaming, to binding relatedness in a love relationship.

To summarize, Merlin is a personification of the wise old man who is closely united with nature, and his visionary capacities can be understood as sight, imagination, and intuition. What, then, does the nymph Viviane embody?

Tradition says of her that she is learned; she knows how to write, and she always retains what Merlin says. But she is also obligated to Diana, the moon goddess, who protects springs and streams. She has access to what springs and streams forth from the unconscious; she is responsible for the protection of this springing and streaming forth. She is connected to the earth but in a lighter manner than Merlin; she is not imprisoned by the earth.

Thus Viviane could be a model for a woman who feels herself obligated to Diana, the goddess of the forest and of nature, and who participates in the natural wisdom and sight of this female deity and in the abundance of life. Viviane could be a model for a woman who knows about her nature, her body, her desires, her eros, but also about the power of inner images and of their waxing and waning. She is learned and lives her eros in a relationship to a wise old man, whose wisdom and vision of life she lets live as well. In doing this she does not become a wise old woman but embodies a wisdom that perpetually renews itself in connection with nature. She is also a woman who can actively engage her abilities—also those she has learned from Merlin—according to her will.

Merlin can be rejuvenated and live on through her in a transmuted form; Viviane unites the realm of the Great Mother with the realm of Spirit; both are expressed and lived in their love for each other. The danger lies in Merlin's remaining caught. Or does our experience say more precisely that he remains caught only in his old form but that in his new form he already lives on in Viviane?

Yet there remains a problem. In magic, in the capacity of imagination to effect change, there is also a danger of enchanting something, of no longer letting go, of using power inappropriately. This danger cannot be abolished; we must live with it. Images can also have a captivating power, as when we imagine a future situation that we perceive with anxiety, and in the actual situation we cannot free ourselves of this image, even if it no longer fits reality.

Images must remain "in motion," that is, we must leave them to their natural rhythm; then they come and go—just as Merlin again and again appeared and disappeared. As soon as we have the feeling that we must "do" something with these images, make use of them, get a grip on them, hold onto them beyond their time, they become constrictive. Just as these imaginings are springs of the greatest wisdom and indeed can give us a certain insight and second sight, they can also cast a spell if imagination is no longer an expression of our deepest nature but rather a reflection of petty demands of the ego.

In the fantasies of relationship I have presented, I have attempted to demonstrate how much the imagination plays a role in love, how much a love stimulates our fantasy, how much we see the beloved person's best possibilities and love forth those best possibilities from him or her. But we also fantasize our own best possibilities in relationship to this beloved thou, and through the imagination they become reality; through a thou we become more ourselves and yet remain in the relationship, and thus we also abolish our separateness from one another.

Merlin's withdrawal into the forest and his union with Viviane indicate a spiritual turning point: The great wise man's, seer's, magician's, psychopomp's way of working has changed. His place is no longer at the court of the king and in the world of success but rather in the world of love and relationship. He is enchanted, as the old tale tells us. The question is then put to us: Can we loose the spell, can we live what is expressed in him in a new form—in the form of Viviane, who, as we know, is inseparable from him?

Merlin and Viviane in a Young Woman's Active Imagination

In the following example I would like to show how Merlin and Viviane can be experienced in the imagaination of a contemporary person and can also serve as a model for relationship. The following account reflects the active imagination of a young woman of twenty-five:

> I am sitting in a lush, green forest; the light is playing on the water of a pond, following how the leaves on the trees move gently in the wind. I gaze into the water; I am completely enchanted by the sparkling light. Out of the sparkling light, figures of people arise whom at first I only intuit. Do I dare to see them, to name them?
>
> I want to run away. But I also want to hold my ground. On the surface of the water, a young nymph is dancing, with legs and feet, a wonderfully beautiful body, long, reddish-blond hair. Across from me I discover an old man with a pure white beard and lively, dark eyes, all indicating an old man—and yet he's young. The nymph dances up to him, puts her arm around his neck, and kisses him.
>
> This nymph begins to bother me tremendously. I want to speak with the strange man; I have the need to get in touch with him. Somehow his eyes say to me that he sees something, and I would so very much like to see it, too. But this nymph has ensnared him and seems to have some claim to him; and he, too, seems completely satisfied to be with her. What ever can I do?
>
> If only I had never seen this stupid nymph; and it was I who visioned her forth from the water.
>
> While I'm raging to myself, the image of the couple gets more and more distant. That is obviously the wrong way to deal with them.
>
> I hear the man laughing, a very relaxed laughter. I know that I must bewitch the nymph; otherwise I'll never get close to this man.
>
> How do you bewitch nymphs? She takes no interest in me; that's unthinkable.
>
> I wonder if I could vision forth a handsome young prince from the water for her? I doubt that I can do that, and then I also doubt whether she is approachable that way.
>
> I gaze into the water. I concentrate on the depths and wait for something or someone to show itself to me. But everything remains calm; only the two of them are

mirrored in the water, and I realize that exactly what I must not do is to get rid of the nymph, but that I must address them both as a couple.

Now they have come closer again. About them is an atmosphere of secrecy and tenderness, of wisdom and eros, and also a little bit of infamy. Basically that comes from the nymph, but that must also apply to the wise old man, for how else could he be with her?

This couple, seen in active imagination, resembles Viviane and Merlin, and the scene takes place in their "domain of life." The young woman obviously has no trouble with the old man, but with the nymph she does have difficulties. The solution for her is to see them as a couple.

A year later this woman was involved in a relationship to an older man, whom she saw as a wise old man. Through her he was rejuvenated and felt that he could pass on in concentrated form everything that he had experienced and learned. He called her "little nymph," which she did not like, but it was an expression that seemed to capture her seductive, erotic, and mysterious aspects. He loved her connection to nature, which was so natural to her that she was not even conscious of it; he loved her groundedness in herself and her natural intelligence. Through his imagining all these characteristics, he loved forth these characteristics in her, but he also developed them in himself. He also felt "more ground" under his feet, yet the weight of groundedness did not oppress him too much. She learned to love the nymph in herself. He loved her capacity for enthusiasm, and through her he became capable of enthusiasm again.

She loved the man's wisdom, his knowledge of life's greater interconnections, his confidence in dealing with everyday life, his calmness. In him she saw a man with prophetic talents and with an understanding of the laws of the unconscious, and she was eager also to understand them. She accepted him as guide in the world of the unconscious and in the world of spirit. He awakened in her the longing for everything spiritual and for the creative, which has to do with soul and spirit. Through her love and her admiration, she "forced" him to examine once again what he really did think and believe. After this happy beginning and a very fulfilled phase, the relationship became difficult; the old man fell ill and withdrew, although with gratitude for once again having experienced something very beautiful.

But even before he had withdrawn, the feeling had come over the young woman that the time of prophets and wise men had already passed. She simultaneously developed a very intense relationship to a figure in her dreams whom she called Merlin. The first phase of this imaginary relationship was concerned primarily with Merlin's telling her everything that she did not know. This sort of active imagination eventually got boring, and she temporarily forgot Merlin.

In a second phase this inner Merlin awakened a tremendous longing for everything that lay beyond waking consciousness. She meditated, became moody, somnambulistic, and yet she was quite satisfied.

In a third phase she could no longer give herself over to these active imaginings and moods, and she began to give them form. She found out that she could yield to the active imagination, that many interconnections became clear to her, and that these imaginings also fulfilled her; but she also perceived that she had to take a critical stance toward these imaginings: She had to confront the unlivable with the livable. It was no longer so much a wanting to know, a wanting to master, as a kind of seeing arising from a loving connectedness with people and things.

For the young woman, the old man was her bridge to this new possibility of living as a person in the world, a possibility which was connected on the one hand to the body, reality, eros and sexuality, and on the other to life from the depths and trust in intuitions and inner images. For the old man, she was stimulation and the concentration of his life experience, but he also had to let go of her, and he hoped that he would live on in her to some extent.

The story of this relationship shows how the Merlin-Viviane union can be experienced in projected form in a human relationship, as well as lived. The young woman had to separate what she called "Merlin in herself" from the real man, and she had to live this Merlin in herself as an inner possibility; the real man, however, had lured forth in her this possibility of life. The Merlinic elements in this story are that she is sent off on her own path (the quest for the Grail), she learns to live in the imagination and to trust it, and she learns to stand in good connection to nature and to all natural things.

Hatem and Suleika: The Theme in Goethe's Writings

A further relationship between an old man and a young woman is presented in Goethe's *Der West-östliche Divan* [*West-Eastern Divan*] which contains the "Book of Suleika," love poems that have a unique place in world literature.[12] At the home of Johann Jakob Willemer, the sixty-six-year-old Goethe meets Willemer's young wife, Marianne. He falls in love with her and expresses his feelings for her in verse, his usual way of expressing love for a woman.

But now something unexpected happens to him, according to Maltzahn: "Marianne replies the very next day in verse that repeats the flow and the rhyme of his verse and thereby shows, more than through the content, how she has adopted his essence—not only of the person but especially of the poet."[13]

Goethe gave Marianne the name "Suleika"; in an Arabic legend she is the unattainable beloved of Joseph. Goethe knew well that this love had come into his life too late to be lived, although Marianne was ready "to disregard all external and coventional hindrances." After a few weeks during which these "lyrical confessions of love" were exchanged, he fled to Heidelberg. They never saw each other again.[14]

It is fascinating that through this love, Marianne became a poet but again fell silent when the relationship ended. The poet was able to love forth from her the poetic side; through his love he brought to life her creative power.

The poems in the "Book of Love" and the "Book of Suleika" in the *West-Eastern Divan* are the expression of this love.[15] I would like to quote some of these poems, which portray the relationship of an old man to a young woman from the viewpoints of Goethe and Marianne Willemer.

That Suleika by Joseph was delighted
Does not surprise:
He was young, youth wins the prize;
He was fair, they say he was entrancing,
Fair was she, bliss for each other enhancing.
But now that you, whom I have so long awaited,
Youth's burning glances send me like this,
Love me now and later give bliss,
This all my songs shall praise and acclaim,
You'll bear always Suleika's name.

Now you bear Suleika's name
I too need a name to be.
When your lover you would acclaim
Hatem! that's what the name should be. . . .

In the phrase, "whom I have so long awaited," Goethe expresses how long he has waited for her, and for the transports of love she sets free in him.

Hatem.   Thieves occasion does not make
            Which itself commits great theft;
            All love's remnants it did take
            Which within my heart were left.

            All my life's accomplishment
            It has put into your hand,
            Now in my impoverishment
            Life depends on your command.

            But already in your eye
            I see mercy's glowing jewel,
            In your arms embraced I lie
            Sensing fortune's glad renewal.

Suleika.   By your love I am elated,
            With occasion find no faults:
            Theft on you was perpetrated,
            How such theft my joy exalts.

            And why should we speak of thieving?
            Give yourself with open eyes;
            All too much I like believing:
            I it was took you as prize.
            What you gave at cost so small
            To such splendour it matures;
            All my peace, rich life, my all,
            I give gladly; all is yours!

            Do not jest! No thought of alms!
            Does not love have such rich sequel?
            When I hold you in my arms
            Mine is every fortune's equal.

Here Goethe expresses that he has given all his "life's accomplishment" to her; these accomplishments are the riches of an old man. And Marianne Willemer, who wrote the poem "By your love I am elated," is likewise ready to give him all her riches. She does not want to hear anything of thieving and taking but rather of giving to each other from their abundance.

The feeling of richness that love evokes is beautifully expressed in this exchange of love between an old man and a young woman.

Suleika.   The sun appears! Such splendour sighted!
            The sickle moon embraces now.
            Who could this pair have so united?
            This puzzle how explain it? How?

Hatem.   The Sultan could; 'twas he who mated
            This highest couple hand in hand,
            Thus his elect he designated,
            The bravest of his loyal band.

> Our bliss is imaged here the clearest!
> Now you and me again I see.
> Your sun you call me, you my dearest,
> Come close, sweet moon, enclosing me!

Here they both express their fantasy: the union of sun and moon. They see their lives cosmically as the fortunate embrace of two principles of life, which together express a totality but which cannot actually come together. It seems to me that a Shiva-Shakti fantasy, the symbolic union of every great love, is expressed here in cosmic symbols, as is the sense of astonishment that such a thing is possible at all. Hatem appeals to the most sublime universal couple, whose secret of love he senses in his relationship to Suleika. These verses imply that the divine aspect shines through in every human love and that each of the two lovers grows beyond himself or herself.

Hatem.   Love for love and hour for hour,
          Look for look and kiss for kiss;
          Word for word, most faithful power,
          Breath for breath and bliss for bliss,
          So this evening, so tomorrow!
          Yet you feel my songs implying
          Ever still a secret sorrow;
          Could I Joseph's charms but borrow
          To your beauty so replying.

Suleika.   Nations, ruler, slave subjected,
          All on this one point agree:
          Joy of earthlings is perfected
          In the personality.

          Every life is worth the choosing
          If oneself one does not miss;
          Everything is worth the losing
          To continue as one is.

Hatem.   May be so! the text is cited;
          But another track I see:
          I find all earth's joy united
          In Suleika, only she.

          Lavish she gives me her substance
          That I value me to be;
          Instantly I'd lose existence
          Should she turn herself from me.

Nevertheless, Hatem is worried that he cannot do justice to her youth; he would love to be the appropriate partner for her. Suleika comforts him: If one does lose oneself, one can lead any life. But Hatem—the old man—confesses that he would lose himself instantly if she were to turn away from him. Here it is revealed how deeply he has lost himself in this love, how he has let himself be seized by love, and how his experience of himself depends on this love. Matzahn observes that in Goethe's diary "after the note that he has written the farewell letter we find only one single Arabic character, which, translated, means: 'I scream from torture.'"

But things have not developed to that point yet; Goethe is still savoring the miracle that even as an old man, he can be loved:

Hatem.   In the circle of her features
Tresses, hold me firmly caught,
I can't answer you dear creatures,
Tawny serpents, I have nought.

This heart only keeps its flower,
Holds youth's ever-flooding urge,
Under snow and mist and shower
Feel an Etna rage and surge.

You make blush, like red of morning,
This high summit's dour retreat,
And once more there comes to Hatem
Breath of spring and summer's heat.

Waiter here! The bottle flashes!
Now for her this glass shall be!
Should she find a heap of ashes
She'll say: "That one burned for me."

Suleika.   Love shall give to love its power,
I shall lose you nevermore!
To my youth you bring the flower
Of your passion strong and pure.
Ah! to my own heart alluring
When they praise my poet's merit!
Since all life is love maturing,
And the life of life is spirit.

Once again Goethe savors the entirety of his passion, and Marianne confesses that love gives love its power; she senses that his love, the love of an entire life, can also bring her love to flower. In her joy at this increase in the intensity of life that has befallen her, she gives form to one of the most profound statements about love:

Since all life is love maturing,
And the life of life is spirit.
. . . .
Ah, West Wind, your moist wings gliding
Stir my envious admiration:
For to him you bring this tiding
How I grieve in separation!
Your wings' motion has such power,
Yearning through my heart it presses;
Hill and forest, field and flower
Fill with tears from your caresses.

Yet your mild and gentle blowing
Soothes and cools my eyelids burning;
I had died from pain so glowing
But for hope of his returning.

Hurry then to meet my lover,
Softly to his heart appealing;
Yet you must not cloud him over,
And my pain must keep concealing.

Tell him, though, with modest voice:
That his love is my life's essence,
In them both I shall rejoice
When again I feel his presence.

In this poem, in which parting is again united with the statement that "his love is my life's essence," Marianne conveys that a love so intense should also make parting so painful; she knows no limitation, as indeed true love knows none, either.

In the following poem, Goethe describes reuniting as a creation myth; he equates the experience of oneness and wholeness in love to the creation of the universe.

Star of stars, what explanation!
Pressed against my heart again!
Ah, the night of separation,
Such a chasm, such a pain!
Yes, it's you! to all my pleasure
Sweet and dearest counterpart;
When in thought past grief I measure,
How the present rends my heart.

When the world in deep conception
Lay in God's eternal breast
He so ordered its inception
With sublime creative zest,
And the word: "Become!" was spoken;
With resounding painful shout
Then the One, by power broken,
To reality thrust out.

Light appeared! immediately
See the darkness parting shy,
Elements each separately
From each other further fly.
Swift, in fierce wild dreaming legions,
Each leapt out to distance bound,
Rigid, through unmeasured regions,
With no yearning, with no sound.
God was first alone that morrow,
All was silent, still, forlorn:
Then to love and comfort sorrow
He created red of dawn;
Colours through the gloom vibrated,
Harmonies resolving pain,
All that first was alienated
Now once more could love again.

All belonging seeks its pleasure,
Swift towards itself returns;
And to life which has no measure
All that sees, all feeling turns:
Seizing, snatching, all unheeded
If it only grips and holds!
Allah's labour's no more needed,
In ourselves his world unfolds.

So on dawn's red pinions soaring
I was torn your mouth to feel,
Night our union makes enduring,
Starbright thousandfold shall seal.
On this earth we are forever

Paragons in joy and pain;
And the word: "Become!" shall never
Separate us once again.

Yet Goethe parts from Marianne because he recognizes that in terms of his stage of life, this love has come too late to him. What it meant to Marianne we do not know; she fell silent, or her poems were lost. In her poem "Ah, West Wind," it is clear how greatly even a temporary parting hurt her.

The "Book of Suleika" ends with a poem by Goethe:

Though you to hide in thousand forms discover,
Yet, All-beloved, you at once I see;
With veils of magic you yourself may cover,
All-present-being, you at once I see.

When cypress thrusts with youth's pure tremulation,
All-beauty-formed, you at once I see;
And in canal's pure living undulation,
All-pleasing-soft, you full well I see.

When soaring fountain waters are ascending,
All-playful-one, how joyful you I see;
When cloud its moving form mutates unending,
All-manifold, you therein I see.

On veil as meadow lawn with flowers spangled,
All-starlight-sparkling, lovely you I see;
In ivy's thousand clasping arms entangled,
O All-embracing-one, you there I see.

And when on mountains morning strikes and blazes,
You, All-things-brightening, I greet at once;
Above me sky its vault pure rounding raises,
All-heart-expanding-one, then you I breathe.

From outward sense, and inner, all my knowledge,
You All-instructing, I know all through you;
The hundred names of Allah I acknowledge,
With every name there echoes one for you.

For Goethe, the entire world becomes transparent through the woman he loves, the beloved Thou; she appears to him in everything, and the beautiful names he gives her convey her omnipresence: "All-beloved, All-present-being, All-beauty-formed, All-pleasing-soft, All-playful-one, All-manifold, All-starlight-sparkling, All-embracing-one, All-things-brightening, All-heart-expanding-one, All-instructing." These names make clear how much she embodied the whole of what he can comprehend and love. She is his one and all, the entire intensity of his feelings. The imagination that amplifies Marianne and transforms her into a goddess becomes visible.

These are poems that describe the essence of love, its heights, its expanses that reach into the absolute, the pain of parting. Through Goethe's love for Marianne, the entire passion of his life once again breaks forth in him, but it is made more intense by his certainty that this love cannot be lived for long. Goethe includes his rich *Weltanschauung* in this relationship. Marianne is seized by this passion and discovers her greatest creative possibilities in the service of her great love. The forced break in the relationship is typical of the older man/young woman constellation. Seldom can this pattern of relationship be so fully lived that it transforms into a new form of relationship.

Montauk: The Theme in the Works of Max Frisch

Max Frisch's books often depict relationships in which older men fall in love with young girls, as, for example, in his story, *Montauk*. In this story, the narrator consciously and with difficulty resists the temptation of wanting to become young again through a relationship to a younger woman. "He knows his age; he is resolved finally to accept it." He does not intend to take her in. His involvement with her evokes in him memories of his relationships with various women and allows him to relive them emotionally and sometimes to value them. It is as if all of his relationships to women are mirrored in this older man/young woman constellation. Thus he finally asks himself whether his love is really intended for Lynn, perhaps every love also contains all the loves one has experienced in a lifetime.

In the end, they part from each other—as foreseen—without pathos. Each is indebted to the other for memories, adventures, experiences. A possible dependence is carefully avoided; Lynn explicitly retains her autonomy, and the writer does not intend to repeat his earlier mistakes in love.

In this story, the aspect of remembering is important; through his love for a young woman, the older man remembers all of the relationships that filled his lifetime or that burdened it with guilt. For this man, the relationship is a condensation of all his love experiences but also an occasion to see his life as a whole and thus also to come to terms with age.

The Model of Older Man/Young Woman as Resolution of the Zeus-Hera Relationship

It is time to return to the conflictual couple mentioned at the beginning of this chapter who illustrate the Zeus-Hera constellation. Although this couple had developed fantasies of older man/young girl and older woman/young man, they continued to battle each other. One day the wife admitted a longing that lead beyond the old cliché: "I get furious that you always make me assert myself rather than let me be devoted." The husband replied that he would also like to have a different style of relationship; he was tired of their conflict, but she made him continue asserting himself.

Following this conversation they initially felt a profound sense of powerlessness. They wanted to change the situation, but they could not. This sense of powerlessness, which I as a therapist shared (I, too, had long felt powerless), stood in the room and was experienced in silence. At that moment, we did not even have words at our command, and in such a power-based relationship, that silence really meant something. Experiencing this situation and enduring the powerlessness were very important and introduced a new phase.

At the end of the hour I suggested to them that from now on they view the battling couple—a label that applied to their entire life together—as an intrapsychic conflict, that is, as two opponents in their own souls who were continually battling each other. They should call them "Zeus" and "Hera" so that they themselves could gain some distance from these fighting partners. Every real conflict outside that might take place between them should be simultaneously waylaid as an inner conflict, refought, or, if possible, even prefought—if it reappeared outside—so that it would not have to be stalwartly battled in their relationship to each other. Instead, it could be dealt with between Zeus and Hera in the fantasy of each.

I suggested that they see their mate as an aspect of and as a fellow player in the fantasy of relationship. Both had sufficiently recognized that they entangled each other in these escalating conflicts. For me it was an attempt to integrate the form of relationship that they no longer wanted to live, assuming that a new fantasy of relationship could only start to function when the old one no longer really functioned. In this case the old relationship had lost its purpose because it no longer guaranteed the optimum closeness along with the greatest degree of separateness.

Each person fought "inner" arguments. The wife's argument looked something like the following:

My Hera says: You are always so power-hungry, Zeus, you'll destroy me.
My Zeus says: I destroy you only because you always want to destroy me.
My Hera says: That isn't true.
My Zeus says: That is true.
My Hera says: See, you're power-hungry again . . .

Each time she soon quit the fantasy because she found them boring and was also ashamed to talk about them in her therapy hour.

The husband's argument was as follows:

My Zeus asks: Why do you do that, Hera?
My Hera answers: Because you always want to decide things for me, because you have taken away my dignity as a woman, because you won't let me make any decisions, because you do not see where I can give you something, too, because you do not love me.
Hera asks Zeus: Why do you do that, Zeus?
Zeus to Hera: Because I am afraid, because I feel powerless and yet I must be Zeus, because it is so difficult for me to be really independent.

In his imaginary argument the husband reveals that he has heretofore devalued his feminine side and that he has had great difficulty maintaining his Zeus-like image.

Through these imagined arguments, both spouses were stimulated to see the conflict between them as primarily a conflict within their own person. The husband could better formulate the conflict than could the wife; she clearly saw how both sides in her demanded equal strength and power.

I hoped that through these fantasies they would both be able to integrate their old form of relationship so that they could then live a new form with a new fantasy of relationship. These exercises, which they each did primarily at home, did bring about a great change in their dynamics as a couple. Both of them attempted to avoid arguing because they found the exercises that they had to do right after an argument difficult. They also started to talk to each other about how often they had to do the exercises and what feelings they had when they did.

One day the husband happily told me how suddenly they could talk to each other and could really listen to each other. They consoled each other, too, whenever the one or the other was suffering because the exercise had to be done again and again or because their fantasies were so desperately similar. The husband said, "Whenever she despairs that this Zeus-Hera business will never stop in her, then she seems to me like a young girl whom I can comfort about it.

I like her in this role very much, but I can also easily let her comfort me."
From this comment we can see how both of them were gradually beginning to live according to a new model of relationship; they now began to live out with each other the pattern of older man/young girl that had appeared in the husband's fantasy. (The pattern of older woman/younger man was much less distinctly realized in the relationship.) In this pattern of relationship, they could both retain power even if they alternated in their use of it. Their closeness was also preserved, but they did not have to set their limits so compulsively.

The husband felt very good in this phase; he found that now he could be strong and weak, too, as he needed; he no longer had to assert himself doggedly. Various problems that they had not resolved for years now found solutions. For the husband the only difficulty was that in this phase he felt very attracted to younger women and would have liked to have had an affair with one of them, but he did not want to do that to his wife.

The wife showed concern for the "infants" she had dreamed about; they had represented possibilities of living that needed to be nurtured in order to grow, and they had also conveyed her need for tenderness. The wife's new awareness of her needs created a change in her pattern of behavior. For example, one day when they were about to battle in the old way, the wife said, "I don't want to fight with you at all; I want to be understood and caressed by you."

But a new crisis was in the making: The wife reacted with greater hostility when her husband treated her like a daughter. In this pattern of older man/ young girl, the husband strongly emphasized the father-daughter aspect, which of course this constellation contains. Because of the wife's strength, vitality, and new awareness of her needs, she reacted with increasing sensitivity to her husband's tendency to spoil her but also to curtail her autonomy. When she revealed her need for tenderness, however, she invited him to spoil her. She felt that she was falling more and more into the role of the daughter. She talked about wanting to have a genuine partnership, but he felt rejected by this demand; in his opinion, they did have a real partnership and could now find appropriate solutions to most of their problems. He was afraid that she, because of her dissatisfaction, would revert to the former Zeus-Hera pattern.

The wife was also aware of this, and to avoid falling back into the patterns of their conflicted marriage, she pondered a separation. The husband reacted with fright; he converted his fright into the threat that he would pull the purse strings if she left him. This threat, in turn, made the wife feel like she really was a daughter dependent on father, and she did not want that under any circumstances. Moreover, a new problem arose for the wife: She began to be bored with their sex life.

Inner Separation

In a relationship it is possible to experience an inner separation from the partner without this leading to an external separation. Often it is wise in a marriage to draw back into oneself and attend to one's own needs, even if that withdrawal is experienced by the partner as a separation that produces sadness and anger, much as an external separation would. The inner separation differs from the external only in that initially the couple remains together and must repeatedly give each other signs about where each is in the process, what issues occupy each at the moment, where each stands vis-à-vis the fundamental issue constellated at the moment, how the fantasy of relationship looks, and so forth. I tried to explain to the conflictual couple that it is unthinkable that two persons could live out the changes in their relationship in full synchrony and that they were tremendously fortunate that their Zeus-Hera phase had ended at about the same time.

At this time the wife formulated the problem this way: "Sure, he's very nice, but he dominates me; for him I remain a daughter. Of course, I am a mother, but that is always only temporary. I don't want to be that, either. I want to be an equal, a partner. And the partnership shouldn't be like Zeus and Hera anymore, but friendly, tender, but with equal rights and excitement, too. If I can't live that with him, then I will with some other man."

The husband described the relationship this way: "I don't see any problem at all. I find that we now have a good relationship. And I don't dominate my wife. I don't understand how I could be different; I feel fine. But now I feel very much criticized again, so of course I could fall back into the Zeus role. I am in favor of a cordial, tender partnership, but we already have that, you see."

While his wife looked for a new fantasy of relationship and inwardly distanced herself from her husband, he felt robbed; he had the feeling that after so much effort, he was now being abandoned, and he attempted to press me into the role of the mother who consoles her son. He also tried to hinder the change with a threat that he could revert to the Zeus role. But nobody was afraid of Zeus. On the contrary, his opposition to the change helped his wife distance herself from him and clearly see what she wanted. Through his opposition she could now disavow the fantasies of relationship they had both lived to this point and set her own limits.

It is easy to empathize with her husband's reaction: The mate who still feels comfortable in the fantasy of relationship sees no reason to change anything. The other's desires for change that are expressed in new fantasies are experienced as a disturbance, as punishment, or at least as the expression of the partner's dissatisfaction.

They were reluctant to take up my suggestion that they accept this as a time of inner separation and learn to let go of each other but also to live with their loneliness in a dyadic relationship, to mourn what was lost, and to hope that a new rapprochement would be possible. The wife was reluctant because she wanted to leave; the husband was reluctant because he wanted me to make his wife listen to reason and to reestablish the old conditions.

I was able to convince them that it was wise to view this crisis as a separation within the relationship; that is, to perceive and work through the separation that actually existed. I also encouraged them to think about what they had always wanted to do if their mate had not prevented them and to use this as a time to realize their desires.

I also guided them during the process of working through this inner separation. They needed to perceive their feelings of abandonment and all the corresponding emotions and to sense what each of them lacked when their mate was only minimally attentive and emotionally present. They were supposed to discover which parts of their souls no longer felt addressed and then ask themselves whether they could bring these feelings of vitality into their own lives or whether they could experience them only through the presence of their mate. I also asked them to let new relationship fantasies arise.

This phase lasted about four months. The wife realized that she viewed her husband as a hindrance, even if he had no idea of what she was doing and actually did not hinder her. She was also struck by how easily she got into a daughter role as soon as a moderately impressive man approached her. She saw this pattern of behavior, got angry about it, and realized that she shared this pattern with many other women.

She cultivated relationships with women and felt that her problems were understood by these female friends. She realized that many of her problems were really problems of an entire generation. But she missed her husband's attention, which had given her "meaning," as she said. She found it difficult if not impossible to give herself this attention. It was thus the attention and meaning that her husband had given her that were important to her. It was striking that she now spoke of attention; previously she had spoken of "control." She missed the tenderness they had experienced together in the preceding phase, and she missed being able to make him beam: "He can beam so that I feel like a magician."

During this phase of inner separation, the couple had maintained a common household with their three children but otherwise they approached each other minimally. Yet the woman had discovered many things during this time: Her husband brought meaning to her life; they could be tender to each other; she had the "magical" ability to make him smile. In the few conversations they had during this time the wife continually attempted to make clear to her husband how much she wanted him to change so that they could really live together again.

Initially the husband got depressed, caught the flu, recovered badly, and the doctor sent him away to recuperate. The treatment pampered him and did him good; he made friends with some men and began to play a sport that his wife had flatly rejected. He recognized that his pampering of himself was also something important. A man who is so invested in the Zeus role is naturally one who demands a great deal from himself in terms of accomplishment and endurance.

Because the inner separation had also become an outer one for him, his grief work became much more existential. He began to miss his wife, who visited him regularly, but in a "separated" way; he missed her way of challenging him and sensed that her mixture of aggression and eros greatly stimulated him and brought out his vitality. At the same time he was also happy that she was not there because he felt less challenged that way. He could thus sink into dullness in peace, but he began to realize that he could not get out of that state by himself; he could not summon the vitality in himself that his wife could elicit. "She makes me lighter," he said, "and increasingly I lack that." He became aware that as soon as he was no longer totally certain whether his wife "appreciated" him enough, he tried to dominate her and coerce love.

Now he was able to ask himself whether she might perceive him to be like a father in these situations. He also missed the erotic aspects of their relationship. But he always feared that if he told her all of this, he would be admitting that he needed her. He wondered whether he would then feel "put upon" again.

A fellow patient at the sanitarium greatly helped the man by pointing out that phrases like "dominate" and "put upon" point to an antiquated system that only knows of superiors and inferiors but not of persons who live and let live. This fellow patient made it his purpose for the moment to wean the man of these concepts and of the thoughts and behaviors that go with them; he was at least partially successful in this endeavor.

Now the husband also began to form new fantasies of relationship that involved his new way of thinking and his needs: "I see myself and my wife taking a walk in the foothills of the Alps. We are both buoyant. Sometimes we take the same path, sometimes we go separate ways, however we feel at the time. Each time we meet again, we beam at each other and are happy." In his fantasy both of them were young and attractive. The fantasy expresses the longing for a true partnership. This form of relationship includes separation, respects the needs of both persons for autonomy, and expresses the joy of encountering each other again and again.

The wife found this fantasy to be very stimulating. The man's fantasy of the stroll in the foothills of the Alps approached her fantasy of the imagined mountain climb with the young man. She suggested that they could also try to look at the father-daughter pattern of relationship as an intrapsychic problem they each had to work on, just as they had worked on and eventually integrated the Zeus-Hera pattern. She would assume responsibility for the fatherly and the daughterly in herself; he should do the same thing, since the mother-son model of rearing was scarcely apparent. For the wife this meant that she must recognize when she let herself be turned into a daughter; she resolved to let this daughterly side also live but to care for it once in awhile in a sisterly and motherly way. She also wanted to see when she slipped into a fatherly role, but instead of longing for a father who would arrange everything for her and whom she would later criticize, she wanted to assume responsibility for her actions.

The husband was supposed to recognize when he ran the danger of playing father or wise old man for her and to try to avoid the situation or make them both aware of it. He was also supposed to allow himself to experience his daughterly, "softer" side. Both were ready to look at this pattern of relationship as an intrapsychic drama as well, but often in their daily life they could not avoid seducing each other into playing the old game.

For example, the wife had to give a report in her women's group. She had not given a report since she left school. She asked her husband how she should do the report. He was overjoyed and began to list various points, and then he pulled out some books. She got furious and said, "Now you are browbeating me again, now you are treating me like a daughter." He was hurt and angry: "But you yourself asked for help. And when I give you help, then I'm browbeating you. . . ." Then she said, "I asked for help, but I don't want *that* kind of help." They fought again as they had in the old days until they realized that they had both slipped into the father-daughter pattern again.

What had happened? In the wife this wise old man/little girl couple had been activated. She had wanted to give an impressive report that would make everyone marvel at her maturity. But this demand had also constellated in her the young girl who is afraid of so much pressure. She really did run to her husband and demand a father's help from him, and he had to be wise at the same time. He thankfully and readily assumed this role and comported himself as the one who knows everything. Instead of really helping her by perhaps drawing out of her what it was that she wanted to do with her report and what her main points were, he gave her directions. But directions always limit autonomy. They would have to learn to help each other in ways that would encourage them to help themselves.

Chapter 7

BROTHER HUSBAND AND SISTER WIFE

Solidarity and Equipoise

He: "You ravish my heart,
my sister, my promised bride . . . ."
She: "Come my beloved
. . . .
Ah, why are you not my brother . . . ."
—The Song of Songs

The New Form of Relationship

A new phase of relationship for our couple was introduced by a dream the wife had: "I am in a neighboring city. I am looking for my husband who has an apartment or an office in a building there. Why, I don't know. But I do know what door bell I must ring. Yet after I have rung, as if I knew all about this living situation, I want to reassure myself one more time that I have pressed the right button. On the nameplate is written: 'Brotherman.'"

Her husband listened to this dream with an expression of fascination on his face when he realized that the dream was about him. He was very happy that his wife was looking for him, yet he had the feeling, justifiably, that the continuation of this relationship was more important to him than it was to her. Beaming, he said, "If I am your brotherman, than you would be my sisterwife."

And so *brotherman* and *sisterwife* became catchwords for their new roles in a relationship they imagined together. It occurred to them that the husband's fantasy of the couple's stroll in the foothills of the Alps could be fitted into this new fantasy without alteration. The names brotherman and sisterwife became very important to both of them. The words *brother* and *sister* would have excluded too much of the important erotic and sexual aspects of their relationship. (The expression "brother-sister marriage" implies, of course, a marriage in which sexuality plays no role.)

Brotherman and sisterwife expressed for both of them a form of relationship that would allow them to stand by each other without being concerned about domination and subjugation. In this relationship, their brotherly and sisterly qualities would create a very special sort of solidarity. They also fantasized about a closeness that would permit delimitation without either person feeling abandoned: Brother and sister would simply belong together as children of the same parents, even when they would prefer not to admit it.

The terms *brother* and *sister* implied to them that even in the most difficult situations, they could always depend on each other; they could confess their weaknesses to each other and rely on the other's support; they could tolerate separation because the other was dependable. Their fantasy of a relationship based on mutual trust influenced the sexual nature of their relationship: The entire erotic-sexual realm resonated for both of them in the words brotherman and sisterwife. Their fantasy of relying on each other, of giving to each other spontaneously, and of revealing their vulnerabilities enabled them to experience new and vital feelings of security and joy.

They have both been trying to live this fantasy of relationship as fully as possible. Of course they have had relapses, but they try to understand what may have caused these relapses: Possibly they have not dared to formulate their partner's needs or have not perceived needs that are important to the partner.

The wife's dream of brotherman suggests a change in her relationship to the masculine outside of herself, as well as to the masculine and feminine within her own psyche. A consequence of the couple's examination of their relationship in terms of the Zeus-Hera pattern was their discovery that they both have strong masculine and feminine components. The wife had difficulty integrating both aspects of her personality because although she wanted to be strong, she could not acknowledge her masculine side. Within her there raged a battle for her identity. With the brotherman-sisterwife fantasy, she found an inner relationship between the masculine and the feminine in which she felt "balanced" because the masculine did not decide everything nor did the feminine.

Using this couple as an example, I have attempted to show how a change in relationship within a partnership can come about, how much this change depends on which fantasies of relationship dominate the two persons, and whether or not new fantasies of one partner can be shared by the other. The transition from an outlived pattern of relationship to a new one always involves a crisis, yet the crisis itself is an opportunity for the partners to discover anew in a new fantasy of relationship.

I also chose this couple because they seemed typical of many contemporary couples who are seeking new patterns of relationship, and in their search various fantasies of relationship may be active concurrently. Relationships that contain a power dynamic seem common today, perhaps because asserting oneself is seen as much more important than the giving of oneself, the losing of oneself; indeed, perhaps it is viewed as more important than giving in general.

In the brotherman-sisterwife fantasy, perhaps a new form of relationship between people in general is revealing itself. In this new form of relationship, dominance is not intended; instead, it involves companionship between equals who excite each other and shape their relationships creatively. In such a relationship, each gives the other the fundamental security and trust that form the basis of a developing union. In the brotherman-sisterwife fantasy women and men could perhaps come to understand that although we are different, we are actually children of the same life, even if we exist in the form of women and men; perhaps we would then have less mutual distrust and would dare not only to fight but also to love.

The importance of the brother-sister couple for the life of the human community has been attested since ancient times. But aside from the myths with matriarchal structures (for example, the Egyptian Isis-Osiris myth in which Isis is both the mother and the sister of Osiris, and thus there is also sexual love between them), all the other brother-sister tales carry an incest taboo. The importance of this relationship lies in the mutual protection and caring that are independent of erotic-sexual attraction; yet it is precisely the erotic-sexual attraction that can bring these sibling couples to disaster in their relation to each other.[1]

This aspect of mutual protection is expressed especially well in Euripides' drama *Iphigenia*, in which Orestes brings back Iphigenia, who has been banished. Vielhauer is of the opinion that the sibling pair Iphigenia-Orestes conceals the sibling couple Artemis-Apollo.[2] We are not concerned with this sort of sibling couple in the brotherman-sisterwife fantasy, although the characteristic feature of the brother-sister relationship are contained in it (namely the mutual aid, the feeling of always being able to rely on the other, the "existential security," and the feeling of equality between man and woman). Vielhauer proves that even in cultures in which the woman was regarded as property to be sold in marriage, she nevertheless had equal rights within the brother-sister relationship.

In the brotherman-sisterwife relationship, we are concerned with the brotherly and sisterly qualities united with eros and sexuality. From among the mythological couples, however, Isis and Osiris do not seem to me to be the suitable example of this new couple's fantasy because Isis and Osiris' roles in the myth are too unequal, and the myth of the great love goddess with her son-lover resounds too strongly. A brotherman-sisterwife fantasy seems to me best portrayed in the Song of Songs.

Shulamite and Solomon

The Song of Songs was recorded in the fourth and third centuries before Christ. Hartmut Schmoekel points out in his book, *Heilige Hochzeit und Hoheslied* [*Sacred Marriage and the Song of Songs*], that many parallels to the Ishtar-Tammuz myth are to be found in the Song of Songs.[3] The parallels are clear, yet I still have the impression that in the Song of Songs this myth is somewhat reshaped—not distorted—in terms of a brotherman-sisterwife relationship. In this chapter I will discuss the Song of Songs from this perspective.

Shulamite and Solomon address each other as sister and brother, but they also have a wonderful love story. At that time in the Near East, "brother" and "sister" were customary forms of address for a beloved person, yet it seems essential that these designations are used here.

Shulamite and Solomon participate equally in courting, in the songs praising the beloved, and also in their mutual pledges of love. This seems to suggest that the Ishtar-Tammuz myth has been transformed by patriarchal influence and has led to a fantasy of relationship that we are perhaps gradually beginning to honor. The courtship initiative proceeds from the bride. But could an Ishtar have said, "Follow after me"? I do not think so. The following verses from the Song of Songs illustrate aspects of the brotherman-sisterwife fantasy of relationship (references are to chapter and verse in the Jerusalem Bible):

> *The Bride*. Let him kiss me with the kisses of his mouth.
> Your love is more delightful than wine;
> delicate is the fragrance of your perfume,
> your name is an oil poured out,
> and that is why the maidens love you.
> Draw me in your footsteps, let us run.
> The King has brought me into his rooms;
> you will be our joy and our gladness.
> We shall praise your love above wine;
> how right it is to love you.
>
> (1:1–4)

The song of praise between the lovers follows as a thoroughly harmonious, well-balanced dialogue:

He. How beautiful you are, my love,
how beautiful you are!
Your eyes are doves.

She. How beautiful you are, my Beloved,
and how delightful!
All green is our bed.

He. The beams of our house are of cedar,
the panelling of cypress.

(1:15–17)

She. I am the rose of Sharon,
the lily of the valleys.

He. As a lily among the thistles,
so is my love among the maidens.

She. As an apple tree among the trees of the orchard,
so is my Beloved among the young men.

(2:1–3)

The bridegroom courts her, calling her "my sister, my promised bride":

You ravish my heart,
my sister, my promised bride,
you ravish my heart
with a single one of your glances,
with one single pearl of your necklace.
What spells lie in your love,
my sister, my promised bride!
How delicious is your love, more delicious than wine!
How fragrant your perfumes,
more fragrant than all other spices!

(4:9–10)

She is a garden enclosed,
my sister, my promised bride;
a garden enclosed,
a sealed fountain.

(4:12)

Fountain that makes the gardens fertile,
well of living water,
streams flowing down from Lebanon.

(4:15)

She answers his wooing:

Awake, north wind,
come, wind of the south!
Breathe over my garden,
to spread its sweet smell around.
Let my Beloved come into his garden,
let him taste its rarest fruits.

(4:16)

In the Song of Songs Shulamite joyfully describes what she has to give Solomon. She presents herself as a woman with self-awareness and great freedom.

I am my beloved's,
and his desire is for me.
Come, my Beloved,
let us go to the fields.
We will spend the night in the villages,
and in the morning we will go to the vineyards.
We will see if the vines are budding,
if their blossoms are opening,
if the pomegranate trees are in flower,
then shall I give you
the gift of my love.
The mandrakes yield their fragrance,
the rarest of fruits are at our doors;
the new as well as the old,
I have stored them for you, my Beloved.
(7:11–13)

Ah, why are you not my brother,
nursed at my mother's breast!
(8:1)

I interpret the expression, "Ah, why are you not my brother" in the symbolic sense, that is, in terms of a fantasy of relationship, because for her to have been able to kiss a dear brother on a public street without someone's having taken it amiss would not have corresponded to the customs of the times.

The Song of Songs ends with Solomon's pledge of love:

Set me like a seal on your heart,
like a seal on your arm.
For love is strong as Death,
jealousy relentless as Sheol.
The flash of it is a flash of fire,
a flame of Yahweh himself.
(8:6)

No son-lover speaks like this, it seems to me, but rather a man who knows love and death. Thus brotherman-sisterwife seems to be a fantasy of relationship (a utopian one?), which, born out of the Ishtar-Tammuz myth, is reformulated in the patriarchal, Israelite Song of Songs as a relationship of equality between man and woman.

Related Existence

Fantasies of relationship are most vivid and easily recognizable in the relationship of lovers. Lovers joyfully yield to their fantasies and through them are seized and transformed in the depths of their personalities. Their fantasies are set in motion within, and these fantasies can create joy as well as anxiety. Couples' fantasies, especially when they are lived in partnerships, express the explicit and the tacit longings that are bound up with the relationship. If we permit a change in our fantasies of relationship, a longing for a perpetually living relationship is expressed in them; this relationship must change, just as life continually changes.

The "leave-taking quality" of our existence reveals itself in the necessity for perpetually new fantasies of and longings for relationship. If we have chosen well, we can also share these fantasies and longings with our partner. To have new fantasies of relationship, however, one must also take leave of old patterns of relationship.

Fantasies of relationship represented in the unions of Shiva and Shakti, Ishtar and Tammuz, Zeus and Hera, Merlin and Viviane, brotherman and sisterwife have somewhat different manifestations in each person. These fantasies also seem to exist side by side, but one fantasy may prevail for awhile and appear dominant in a person's behavior in a relationship. These fantasies are to be understood as the expression of the various forms of human relatedness. A Shiva-Shakti fantasy of relationship seems to form the foundation for all couples who are in love, and it is a fantasy that is more or less consciously perceived. A sisterwife-brotherman fantasy seems to be appearing more frequently among couples these days.

These fantasies and their continually changing imagery not only have a place in love relationships but also in all possible relationships and in regard to all possible partners. Persons who are not in love relationships can cultivate very intensive fantasies of relationship. The longing for love can impart a great intensity to these fantasies and fill a person with feelings of wholeness and love. It is not only a living partner who can stimulate us to create a fantasy that allows us to see that partner's greatest potential and to see ourselves in a new light. Encounters with dream figures can set free similar processes, as can figures in literature and in films who impress us. Then it is as though we had waited for someone or something to appeal to a new and vital potential in us.

We all have many possibilities of relationship if we are attuned to them; we are abundantly related to persons and stimuli that set something in us in motion. Our relatedness to the world has to do with our individuation, our process of becoming ourselves, for not all things can excite us to the same degree; rather, we must be approachable and perceive our approachability in order to create this state in our fantasy.

In the broadest sense, fantasies of relationship enable us to hear the call of the world, and in our answer to that call, we shape the possibilities of our personality, which can only really come alive in this relatedness to the world. In our fantasies of relationship we give form to our deepest longings to transcend our separateness from others and to achieve greater wholeness. When our fantasies are not shared by our partner, we feel constrained in our striving for wholeness and the deepest union; the separation that occurs is likewise fundamental, and it again propels the longing for union.

Fantasies of relationship, even when they are not directed toward a specific person, can give us a feeling of the greatest wholeness or express yearning for something in ourselves that promises greater wholeness.

It is love that lends these fantasies wings, so to speak, and love itself is in turn nourished by these same fantasies of relationship. Then it is difficult to distinguish—and probably not necessary to know—whether it is the fantasy or the love come to life through it that brings us a new, vital feeling of wholeness, hope, and creative bliss; we sense that we are in our native home, and through the transcendence of love we seem to escape everything mundane. In such a state of love, we dare all, we feel that we can give all, and these feelings enliven the fantasy of relationship and intensify love.

Through the vitality of love, we feel capable of dealing with the everyday, recalcitrant world, which perpetually opposes and limits us, because we understand it as *one* aspect of human existence and not the whole. We can also deal more lovingly with the recalcitrant and thereby also transform it.

We participate in love, and we participate in everyday life. I do not mean by this that love is primarily a feeling that exists between people. Love is primarily a *feeling of myself*—that is, I am gripped by that which erupts in me—but at the same time this love always seeks union with a Thou, whether it is a love mate, a thing, nature, or God. Love joyfully unites what is separate while preserving our awareness of ourselves as individuals. Love creates relationship, but there are also relationships into which love hardly enters. Love always has an aspect of the unpredictable about it, and also of grace. Relationship—relatedness—is much more sober, much more dependent on an individual's resolve. Entering a relationship, however, can be the first step toward love's unfolding. For to enter into relationship means to open oneself to another, to let a Thou appeal to and understand oneself, to give to and participate with the other. These are facets of love yet do not constitute the essence of love.

By letting oneself be appealed to by another, the fantasies of relationship begin to create the reality of relationship; letting oneself be appealed to again and again, even by an "old" partner in an existing relationship, makes the blossoming of love continually possible.

Stepping into relationship, which corresponds intrapsychically to the flowering of fantasies of relationship, requires a loving attitude. We cannot "make" love, but we can strive for a loving attitude.

Participating in the everyday world and in the world of love corresponds to two attitudes toward life: the "attitude of mastery," as I will call it, and the "loving attitude." In the ideal case these two attitudes are intertwined; in the less than ideal case we slip into one or the other.

When we have a loving attitude, the soul and everything else become valuable in themselves. The loving attitude is attentive, and it enhances and expands everything with which it comes in contact; the loving attitude enables us to give ourselves generously because we need not hoard. With a loving attitude, we can leave the other person free; we are tender in an all-embracing sense. Its gestures are embracing and letting go, caressing—with words, with the hands, with the eyes. The loving attitude enables our imagination to grow and unfold without impediment. It is not "saccharine"; it keeps us open to the emotional dimension, pledged to the truth of the heart, and ever ready to utter disagreements—even aggressively. A loving attitude must not be confused with harmonizing tendencies. The loving attitude intends the Thou, whereas harmonizing tendencies are concerned with the I.

When we have an attitude of mastery, we are focused on settling concerns, making sure that the investment and the return are at least in balance or that the return is greater. Our concern is mastery and utility. When we have a loving attitude, we leave the other person free, but when we have an attitude of mastery, we use the other for our own ends: We measure and ask about suitability, not about abundance. The gestures of the attitude of mastery are those of laying hold of, putting things in their place, pushing and pulling, settling. The attitude of mastery causes our imagination to be concerned with order, accomplishment, closure. With such an attitude, we know how things ought to behave, how the

Thou must behave, but we do not let things grow by empathizing with them. When we have an attitude of mastery, we can easily become manipulative.

If we truly are people who are "in the world" but who are simultaneously "above and beyond the world" (to use an expression of Ludwig Binswanger,[4] to whom I am indebted for stimulating my thought on this topic), we will always participate in both attitudes. It seems to me, however, that we must again learn to value the loving attitude. Hence I give it preferential treatment here; I would like to make it appealing to us.

The loving attitude would make it possible for us not to become destructive and manipulative. It would bring joy and vitality into our lives again. It would also, however, take us into the world of fantasies and enable us to enhance each other, to foster each other, instead of passing each other by. Of course, the attitude of mastery is important, too; even in the most beautiful love relationship, life must be mastered. We quickly become disillusioned with fantasies of relationship when the "magnificent" other fails at life's simplest tasks. Nevertheless, I believe that mastery is practiced much more than lovingness. An "attitude of loving mastery" toward life would be more appropriate if we want to plumb the depths of our humanity and thus become more secure and fulfilled in our relationships.

Fantasies of relationship relate us to a Thou, to the world, but also to our own depths. In them is expressed a dynamic of life that helps us to approach ourselves more closely—through a Thou, through relatedness to a Thou, through the world.

Although we can resolve to open ourselves to each other, to share, to give of ourselves, and to adopt a loving attitude—in other words, to choose relationship and relatedness—the exuberance of love is something we may or may not experience. We can only remain open to this experience, and well we should.

Chapter 8

CRITICAL
APPRAISAL

The Anima and Animus
Concept of C. G. Jung

In the present work I proceeded from the position that anima and animus are archetypes that can be experienced at any time by both men and women. It seems to me that the interplay of anima and animus in each person is of the greatest significance not only in terms of an individual's identity but also in regard to fantasies of relationship, which are essentially an expression of this interplay and which underlie every relationship. This view is based on my long struggle with and reflection on C. G. Jung's concepts of anima and animus, which I would like to sketch here.

It is greatly to Jung's credit that he continually emphasized that "female" elements (anima) exist in every man just as "male" elements (animus) exist in every woman, and that these elements also need to live. Male and female hormones occur in the male and the female body in various proportions; likewise, every human being should live out the "male" and "female" energies inherent in various proportions in the individual. Jung's concept of the anima and animus enabled many persons to accept themselves as they were and not as they should be according to rigid gender stereotypes. These thoughts on the anima and animus have now become active in the collective consciousness; stereotyped roles are being questioned, and thus a collective process of development has begun that is transforming our ways of living together as well as our understanding of families. Today many people accept the view that men can also have the "female" traits of sensitivity and intuition just as women can have the "masculine" traits of autonomy and goal-directed thought.

Jung is justly praised for his contribution to this change in the collective consciousness, but he is also reproached because his concepts of anima on the one hand and animus on the other are so strikingly unequal. In Jung's writings one cannot overlook that for him the anima was something valuable and desirable, whereas the animus was often a source of trouble. Thus women, who have "only" an animus, are in a worse position than men, as women have been ever since Aristotle.

A theory develops not only through people's building and rebuilding it; it also develops through daily use. In the use therapists make of the Jungian anima-animus theory, the theory is sometimes simplified—often falsified—and in this simplification a fundamental assumption is more frequently expressed than in the more differentiated formulation of the theory. In analytic jargon, the anima—except in the case of anima possession—is accorded respect, even reverence. The concept of animus on the other hand, is often used to disqualify a woman's accomplishments: "She just had a good animus." Such an expression means that a woman has lost a great deal of the "feminine." When the word animus is used, a value judgment—"That should not be"—easily creeps in. The criticism implied in the comment that a woman's standpoint is "animusy" can silence a woman who understands this jargon unless she has developed so much autonomy that she questions the jargon, which then naturally suggests her animus again; yet it is precisely the concept of the animus that gives a woman the possibility of living her inherent "masculine" characteristics and thereby gaining more autonomy.

This is a viewpoint that Marie-Louise von Franz, in particular, raised for discussion. In her writings she repeatedly emphasizes the positive aspect of the animus without denying the negative. In her view

> the animus can personify an enterprising spirit, courage, truthfulness, and in the highest form, spiritual profundity. . . . This naturally presupposes that her animus ceases to represent opinions that are above criticism. The woman must find the courage and inner broadmindedness to question the sacredness of her own convictions. Only then will she be able to take in the suggestions of the unconscious, especially when they contradict her animus opinions.[1]

What the man sees in the woman as his shadow, which is also the shadow of the patriarchy, is often designated "negative animus"; or there is talk of a negative animus when a woman makes a demand or a statement that a man does not like. We probably should speak of a negative animus only when the play of energies in the soul has succumbed to it and when only one voice—which is unconnected with the total personality, mannishly demanding, or destructive—gets a hearing. Even then we would always have to clarify whether or not the root of the problem can really be called animus.

In sorting out what animus and anima means, the battle of the sexes continues to be waged despite the processes of growing consciousness of anima and animus, and this battle must, in my opinion, be a part of it when the duality is so strongly emphasized. Consequently it seems to be essential to discuss the anima and the animus concepts not only as Jung understood them but also in the full sense described by von Franz: We must muster the courage to question sacred convictions. Theories that have become a habitual part of daily practice are, after all, sacred convictions.

First I would like to quote some definitions that I have selected from Jung's works that convey his attempts to grasp the meaning of anima and animus.

Anima and Animus: Jung's Definitions

• "Thus anima and animus are images representing archetypal figures which mediate between consciousness and the unconscious."[2] Between these images, a dynamic balance must be striven for.[3]

Animus	Anima
yang principle	yin principle[4]
expansive	contractive
aggressive	receptive
demanding	preserving
sky	earth
sun	moon
day	night
summer	winter
dry	moist
warm	cold
surface	interior

•"If I were to attempt to put in a nutshell . . . what it is that characterizes the animus as opposed to the anima, I could only say this: as the anima produces *moods*, so the animus produces *opinions*"[5]

•"And just as the anima of the man initially consists of inferior relatedness, full of affect, so the animus of woman consists of inferior judgements, or better said, opinions."[6]

•The concept 'anima' is a purely empirical concept, whose sole purpose is to give a name to a group of related or analogous psychic phenomena."[7]

•"The anima is indeed the archetype of life itself, which is beyond all meaning and moral categories."[8]

•The anima "symbolizes the function of relatedness. The animus is the image of the spiritual forces in a woman, symbolized in a masculine figure. If a man or a woman is unconscious of these inner forces, they appear in projection."[9]

•"The animus is the deposit, as it were, of all woman's ancestral experiences of man—and not only that, he is also a creative and procreative being. . . . He brings forth something we might call the . . . spermatic word. Just as man brings forth his work as a complete creation out of his inner feminine nature, so the inner masculine side of a woman brings forth creative seeds which have the power to fertilize the feminine side of man."[10]

It is striking that the older Jung no longer placed the pathological element in the foreground of his animus and anima definitions but rather simply the possibility of life, which lies in each human peculiarity.

The last definition is one that turns up continuously in feminist literature as evidence that Jung's concepts of anima and animus provide man with a yet more inspiring woman, or *femme inspiratrice*, and that Jung, too, denied woman the creative. Indeed, the definition can be understood that way, but if one starts with the idea that man and woman both have anima and animus, then this definition takes on an entirely different meaning. It must also be kept in mind that Jung worked on these concepts around 1920, and they obviously reflected the spirit and limits of those times. It is not Jung whom we should reproach but ourselves if we again subscribe to the prejudices of his day.

Starting with these definitions, which I will supplement with others, what is the common ground of anima and animus?

1. They are images of archetypal figures. The term *archetypal* signifies that in these images an anthropological constant of human experience and behavior is expressed; it is represented in various people at various times, in comparable images and emotions.[11] A constellated archetype, a "living idea," brings about a

development.[12] As anthropological constants, however, they work in each human being, man and woman.

2. They mediate between consciousness and the unconscious but are also personifications of the unconscious.[13] They represent functions that mediate the contents of the collective unconscious to consciousness. The contents that are mediated can be integrated, but anima and animus as the vehicles of these contents cannot.[14] Here the dynamic, creative aspects of the anima and animus archetypes are described. The dynamic-creative aspect, however, is characteristic of every archetypal constellation.[15]

3. The effects of animus and anima on the ego are in principle the same (Jung explains this in terms of irrational moods and opinions):

- they are difficult to eliminate
- the effect is uncommonly strong
- the ego-personality immediately has the feeling of rightness and righteousness
- the cause is projected onto objects and objective situations.[16] (But, as Jung himself says here, this is how all archtetypal images function.)

4. Animus and anima tend to have a positive feeling value (the shadow has a negative tone): "Anima and animus . . . exhibit feeling qualities that are harder to define. Mostly they are felt to be fascinating or numinous. Often they are surrounded by an atmosphere of sensitivity, touchy reserve, secretiveness, painful intimacy, and even absoluteness."[17] (Thus are archetypal images experienced.)

5. When they are unconscious, they are projected, or are met with as projections.

As long as Jung is describing the common aspects of anima and animus, he is basically stating again and again that they are archetypal images with idiosyncratic dynamics. These two archetypal images differ in the following ways:

Animus	**Anima**
1) Projected on males	1) Projected on females
2) Opinions, inferior judgment (Logos)	2) Moods, inferior affective relationship, relating (Eros)
3) Image of spiritual powers in the woman	3) Archetype of life itself, chaotic life urge, nothing but life
4) A creative essence, the generative "word"	4) The function of relationship
5) Through integration it gives female consciousness the power of reflection, consideration, and conscious (objective) knowledge	5) Through integration it gives male consciousness relatedness and relationship[18]
6) A sort of deposit of all woman's ancestral experiences of man	6) A sort of deposit of all man's ancestral experiences of woman[19]
7) Influence of the father	7) Influence of the mother
8) Collective image of man	8) Collective image of woman
9) Collective image of the masculine in the unconscious	9) Collective image of the feminine in the unconscious[20]
10) Imago of the father, brother, son, beloved, heavenly god, Hades	10) Imago of the mother, sister, daughter, beloved heavenly goddess, Baubo, . . .

Animus	Anima
	every mother, every beloved can become the bearer of all these images[21]
11) Spirit, "'window on eternity" . . . . It conveys to the soul a certain 'divine influx' and the knowledge of higher things, wherein consists precisely its supposed animation of the soul."[22] This higher world has an impersonal character: ■ the totality of traditional intellectual and ethical values. ■ products of the unconscious and archetypal ideas	11) "With the archetype of the anima we enter the realm of the gods. . . . Everything that the anima touches becomes numinous—unconditional, dangerous, taboo, magical[23]
12) Compensates female consciousness, i.e., "eros" (placing in relationship)[24]	12) Compensates male consciousness: i.e., "logos" (differentiation, judgment, objective knowledge)[25]
13) "The animus can personify an enterprising spirit, courage, truthfulness, and in the highest form, spiritual profundity. . . . This naturally presupposes that her animus ceases to represent opinions that are above criticism. The woman must find the courage and inner broadmindedness to question the sacredness of her own convictions. Only then will she be able to take in the suggestions of the unconscious, especially when they contradict her animus opinions."[26] The animus also expresses itself in fantasies, active imagination, etc.	13) "If products of the anima (dreams, fantasies, visions, symptoms, chance ideas, etc.) are assimilated, digested, and integrated, this has a beneficial effect on the growth and development ('nourishment') of the soul."[27]

When Jung described animus as "spirit,"[28] he formulated the traditional view that the soul, which enlivens the body and consequently gets lost in sensuality and emotions, must be retrieved from its "lost condition." Here it becomes apparent how dehumanizing philosophical idealism can be: sensual, emotional life is seen as a "lost condition." On the one hand, Jung understands spirit in the traditional sense of humanity's self-discovery, the vital process of differentiation between human beings and the world (structures of the unconscious and the dynamics that are bound up with it). Spirit in this sense is the totality of the intellectual and ethical values that result from this differentiation as they have taken form and will continue to take form in art, religion, ethics, science, and literature. With the "window to eternity," Jung alluded to the third aspect of spirit: God as absolute spirit, who is expressed in the objective and subjective spirit (Hegel).

It is interesting that Jung saw the structures of the unconscious and the dynamics resulting from them as aspects of spirit—as spirit manifested, so to speak;

in another place he spoke in this connection of "a principle of spontaneous movement and activity" transcending consciousness.[29] This definition of spirit is similar
to Bateson's, who designates spirit as "the essential element in what makes things
live."[30] Jung equated "masculine" consciousness with this spirit in all its aspects; in
the woman spirit would be unconscious. Here lies one of the major points of
criticism: What is "masculine" and what is "feminine" consciousness if this distinc-
tion is to be maintained?

A further problem is that, according to Jung, the woman's experience of father
and the paternal principle nourishes an archetypal image, but the experience of
mother and the material is supposed to be closer to consciousness. Presumably
Jung took this position because he assumed that the first projection-making factor
for the son is the mother and for the daughter, the father.[31] Here lies a fundamental
misunderstanding, for the female child likewise has—or until now has had—
her first relationship with her mother and not her father. A female child can
thus project on both the mother and the father, since in our souls we all carry
images of father, brother, son, beloved, heavenly god, chthonic god, as well as
images of mother, sister, daughter, lover, heavenly goddess, and chthonic goddess.

Jung conceived woman's psychology simply as the opposite of man's psychology
to too great a degree, and hence woman's consciousness was called eros compensated by unconscious logos, whereas male consciousness was called logos
compensated by unconscious eros.

I now want to question the sacred conviction that women have no anima but
an animus and that men have no animus but an anima. I have not been able
to avoid this topic in this book. In examining this issue we must take seriously
what von Franz termed the "hints of the unconscious."

It is beyond question that men and women can be attracted by persons of
both sexes and can sometimes grant them a significance that can only be called
"numinous." We then get entangled in relationships, seduce and let ourselves be
seduced, project onto others and experience their projections. Images of the
anima are found in the dreams of men and of women, in fantasies, and in projections that are always linked with fascination and longing: good fairies, witches,
whores, saints, nymphs, and little girls; all are mysterious and unknown, and
they carry us off into the realm of fantasy.

Using Jung's terminology, we would conceptualize such figures in the case of
a woman as "shadow" (here taken as embodying those characteristics that the
conscious ego rejects and does not want to see as aspects of the personality,
usually calling it a "dark" personality) but also as "positive shadow." If they are
especially gripping, they have been called personifications of the self. Here the
self is understood as the "eternal ground of all empirical being, just as the self
is the ground and origin of the individual personality past, present, and future."[32]

It seems more sensible to me to designate these as anima figures for both men
and women, and to take the shadow as that which we really cannot associate
with our self-concept. The great, abstract symbols of true wholeness, which alone
can fulfill Jung's definitions and the mysteries associated with them, would be
reserved for the self.

The images of the animus are also found in the dreams, fantasies, projections,
and stories of both women and men: compelling patriarchs, mysterious strangers,
divine youths, fascinating thinkers, emerging prophets, and lightning-hurling

divinities. In the conventional Jungian view, these figures for a man would be shadow figures or personifications of the self. If they really are numinous figures carrying a powerful dynamism, would it not be more correct to designate them as animus figures, even in the case of a man, and leave the truly shadowy to the shadow and the really great symbols to the self?

In the unconscious we also find couples who exert this strangely fascinating effect on us, who take possession of us and compel us to deal with them: a mother figure with a fascinating young boy, for example, or a mysterious strange man with a mysterious unknown woman. We might use the term "gods" when we speak of them. In the unconscious we find couples as lovers, siblings, and friends. Jung repeatedly described these couples. His intensive studies of alchemy pivot about these couples, about the *mysterium coniunctionis* between Sol and Luna, for example, only that he always equated one of them with consciousness.

Phenomenologically it seems uncontestable that what Jung called animus and anima are actually experienced as images by both sexes, and the emotions and behaviors associated with these images are the same for both sexes. Jung himself continually emphasized that animus and anima are archetypes. As far as I know, he did not speak of gender-specific archetypes.

If anima and animus are archetypes, they would have to occur in both men and women.[33] We use the term *archetypes* only when the qualities of fascination, numinosity, and mysteriousness are involved; these stimulate creative fantasies (or they stimulate the desctructive, if the creative is not accepted), which cause projections and are fateful. Women can have integrated masculine characteristics having nothing at all to do with this quality of the archetypal; the same is true for men in regard to the integration of feminine characteristics.

This is also expressed in dreams: a thirty-two-year-old woman dreamed that a man of her age, blond, wearing jeans, his sleeves rolled up, spit in his hands and said, "Then we'll just spade the garden and plant it." The dreamer was impressed by this man's initiative (she faced a philosophy exam); he represented that side of her that could take the initiative. As an animus figure he would have to carry a different, more gripping emotional quality like that expressed in another dream of the same woman: "A blond man, about my age, is standing at the sea. I look at him. He has eyes that completely mesmerize me, and through them I can see into the depths of the water. He is very close to me and very far from me, and a longing for him seizes me. Although he stands in front of me, he is somehow unreachable. On the bottom of the ocean I see a young woman in chains. I don't want to see her; I think it is only a dream and awake."

This blond young man suggests to me a mysterious, fascinating, and not really comprehensible man who directs her into the depths. In this dream a couple is also depicted—a union of animus and anima, as I would call it—in whom the anima desperately needs to be set free—the anima of a woman!

On the basis of the evidence, we are finding anima and animus figures in the psyches of both men and women, and quite often, it seems to me, they belong together as a couple. The more I have pondered this phenomenon, the more I have been impressed by how often a couple occurs in the unconscious and reflects animus and anima. Colleagues who know of my ideas have also had this experience. By definition anima and animus are archetypes, and they would have to occur in a like manner in men and women.

Consciousness

We must now consider Jung's statement that animus compensates woman's consciousness (eros, "bringing into relationship"), and the anima compensates men's consciousness (logos, "differentiating"). This thesis caused Jung himself some difficulties:

> If, then, Luna characterizes the feminine psyche and Sol the masculine, consciousness would be an exclusively masculine affair, which is obviously not the case since woman possesses consciousness too. But as we have previously identified Sol with consciousness and Luna with the unconscious, we would now be driven to the conclusion that a woman cannot possess a consciousness.
> The error in our formulation lies in the fact, firstly, that we equated the moon with the unconscious as such, whereas the equation is true chiefly of the unconscious of a man; and secondly, that we overlooked the fact that the moon is not only dark but is also a giver of light and can therefore represent consciousness. This is indeed so in the case of woman: her consciousness has a lunar rather than a solar character. Its light is the "mild" light of the moon, which merges things together rather than separates them.[34]

In his book *The Origins and History of Consciousness*, Erich Neumann writes: "The correlation of 'consciousness-light-day' and 'unconsciousness-darkness-night' holds true regardless of sex. . . . Consciousness, as such, is masculine even in women, just as the unconscious is feminine in men."[35] Does a woman's ego-consciousness have a "masculine" character? Must consciousness be "masculine" or "feminine" at all costs? Must everything be divided up and differentiated? Perhaps we are dividing something here that is not divisible, and by doing so, we are creating artificial conflicts.

Can consciousness be "masculine" or "feminine", and what is consciousness actually? We always speak of consciousness as if it were a known quantity, yet consciousness is probably one of the greatest of all marvels. Jung attempted to circumscribe the concept:

- The ego is the "central reference—point of consciousness."[36]
- "Consciousness can even be equated with the relationship between the ego and the psychic contents."[37]
- ". . . the greatest possible range of consciousness through the greatest possible self-knowledge. . . ."[38]

Subsequently he spoke of meditation and its effect: the training of consciousness, the capacity for concentration, attention, and clarity of thought.

It is important to emphasize that by the expression "range of consciousness" we do not mean that one has many contents in consciousness—such as one collects many objects in a bag. Rather, the range of consciousness is expressed by the radius of clarity, the degree of alertness, and the complexity of possible recall of many memories of situations that we have experienced actually or in fantasy. As the extent of consciousness grows, we have more perspectives from which we can approach our life and our problems, but we also have ever greater possibilities for experiencing because we can link new experiences with a rich store of past experiences if we are somewhat aware of them. Range of consciousness is thus a dynamic concept suggesting greater and greater aperture.

Fundamentally, consciousness can be divided into three domains (see Table 1), yet it is obvious that ultimately we do not know what consciousness is, even though we obviously experience it.

Table 1   Domains of Consciousness

Domain	Ego functions	General human possibilities
1. Alert-insensible (alertness of consciousness)	Sensation perception, conceptualization memory, conceptual systems thought; orientation in time, space, to one's self; attention	Involves right and left hemispheres of brain; the right hemisphere enables us consciously to perceive our perceiving
2. Conscious-unconscious (what can be communicated)	Awareness of the flow of consciousness (metaphors: light, clarity)	If Spirit is the living element in life, then consciousness contemplates the movements of Spirit; in consciousness, Spirit would "become aware of itself."
3. Self-aware (ego-complexes/ sense of self)	Consciousness of ourselves (in contrast to how others see us). Reflects the ego-complex	Identity: continues to take shape over course of life (extent of consciousness) relationship inward and outward. Bodily sensations, conception of body, sexual identity. Ideas that belong to oneself; aspects, behavioral possibilities (male and female)

Compensation: Animus and Anima

In terms of the "alert-insensible" (*bewusst-bewusstlos*) domain of consciousness, there can be no differences between man and woman. Pertinent studies support this[39]; moreover, a male "insensibility" can hardly be distinguished from a female "insensibility."

In regard to the "conscious-unconscious" (*bewusst-unbewusst*) domain, the capacity to be conscious of the flow of consciousness can hardly be different in men and women; it is, after all, a distinguishing human potentiality. If it were the case that women possessed this ability less than men—which would have to be proven—this would probably reflect socially determined circumstances, because this ability is regarded as less important for a woman. But the capacity to observe the flow of consciousness is not different in men and in women. Reference to this can be seen in Juerg Willi's work with Rorschach tests.[40] He determined that there were no typically "feminine" or "masculine" interpretations of the test figures. But when he gave the test to a woman and a man together, the woman suffered a general limitation of ego: She lost her overview and became unproductive. The man, however, increased the extent of his overview, reality adaptation, and affect control in the joint test.

The third domain of consciousness, is "self-awareness" (*selbst-bewusst*). Here we must repeatedly distinguish between the possibility of being aware of oneself, which would be an aspect of the "alert-insensible" (*bewusst-bewusstlos*) dimension, and the content of self-awareness. Only the content of self-awareness is molded by concepts that are "feminine" or "masculine." Our gender identity usually corresponds to our biological gender, but because we also have both male and female elements in our organism, concepts that belong to our person always carry the imprint of both sexes.

In my opinion, consciousness as such cannot be designated as "masculine" or "feminine"; consciousness is a human potentiality. The content of our self-awareness, on the other hand, is gender-specific. If the idea of compensation is at all tenable in Jung's terms—namely, that our consciousness, stamped in a gender-specific form, is compensated by a contrasexual element—then our self-awareness could, in my view, be compensated only by the anima and the animus as a couple in each person.

In reflecting on what Jung could have meant when he equated the consciousness of woman with eros ("bringing into relationship") and that of man with logos ("distinguishing, judging"), it occurred to me that Jung could have assigned to woman and to man two fundamentally human potentialities, that of "empathizing" and that of "delimiting," and moreover might have anticipated what we now call right hemispheric and left hemispheric thinking.[41]

Right Hemispheric Thought	Left Hemispheric Thought
Subdominant hemisphere	Dominant hemisphere
Control over left side of body	Control over right side of body
Almost no connection to consciousness (link via the corpus callosum to the left hemisphere)	Connection to consciousness
Almost nonverbal	Verbal
Musical	Linguistic description
Responsive to image and pattern	Ideas
Combining according to visual similarities	Combining according to concepts
Temporal synthesis (concurrent)	Temporal analysis (sequential)
Holistic, imagistic thought	Analysis of detail
Geometric-spacial	Arithmetic and computer-like[42]

The right and left hemispheres participate in all processes of consciousness in everyone. But it is striking that what we call consciousness corresponds to the function of the right hemisphere; indeed, it corresponds in many areas to what Jung called anima. Yet left hemispheric thought cannot be equated with animus, or at least it does not embrace essential aspects of it.

When we want to make the unconscious conscious, however, it seems to me that we utilize the abilities of the right hemisphere. Perhaps we could even relate

the corpus callosum to Jung's transcendent function, for the right and the left
hemispheres are linked via the corpus callosum, and contents of the right hemisphere do become conscious.

But even if Jung had uncovered right and left hemispheric thought with his
animus and anima concepts, his idea of reserving the animus for women and the
anima for men is not tenable. The dominant hemisphere for women is still the
left, and all human beings have two hemispheres.

Anima is continually associated with "feeling." This above all because a storm
of feelings erupts whenever the image of the feminine is projected onto a human
woman. But emotions are involved in all our processes of perception; our emotions modify our perceptions.[43] Hence we always live a personal equation, but
some are more conscious of it than others, and perhaps in this respect women
have learned to be more conscious than men.

If anima and animus are figures that approach all of us from the depths and,
if they are united, bring us a feeling of wholeness, then their relationship to
each other must be of special importance.

Just as anima and animus always incarnate in relationships and thus are probably the most important archetypes because we constantly deal with men and
women, so must the union of anima and animus also be evident in relationships.
But one person does not simply assume the anima role and the other, the animus
role; instead, an entire couple constellation can be experienced in the psyche
of each person. The creative aspect of begetting and giving birth, which is part
of these fantasies, creates a world of relationship but also a new inner world:
We grow beyond ourselves; we can transcend what has come to be.

To give ourselves to these images from the depths, however they constellate,
to shape them in a living relationship and in fantasy and thereby to unite them
is, in my view, more important than defining anima and animus or what the anima-
animus couple can be. Of course, we can only do this if we feel devotion to
these images, if we let them seize us and let what they work in us come to
pass. Seeing anima and animus as a couple constellation would have a therapeutic advantage: We would not have to speak reproachfully of a woman analysand
"caught in the animus"; such reproaches are not therapeutically effective. Instead
we could ask ourselves what female figure would have to join such a male figure
so that she could feel better, more balanced, more satisfied. And then the vital
feeling that is linked with this anima figure could be imagined and also experienced.

The union of animus and anima—intrapsychically or in a fantasy of relationship
in which both meet—will always bring with it a vital feeling of being spiritually
and emotionally inspired, and often it will also bring love.

Notes

Chapter 1   On the Ferry to the Other Shore
1. Leisi (1978).
2. Bloch (1959, p. 378).

Chapter 2   Shiva and Shakti: The Ideal of Complete Union
1. Zimmer (1977, pp. 250–304).
2. Maupassant (1911, vol. 6).
3. Hohler (1980).
4. Leisi (1978).
5. *Ibid.*, p. 14.
6. Frisch (1976).
7. Kast (1982, p. 61).
8. Zimmer (1977, p. 301).
9. Kast (1982, p. 67).
10. Zimmer (1977, p. 304).
11. Kast (1982, p. 71).

Chapter 3   Pygmalion: The Longing To Form a Partner in One's Own Image
1. Ovid (1980, pp. 224ff).
2. Geissler (1955, pp. 72–73).
3. Bachmann (1978, vol. 3), pp. 402–13.

Chapter 4   Ishtar and Tammuz: The Goddess of Love and her Youthful Lover
1. Schmoekel (1955, p. 7).
2. Goettner-Abendroth (1980, p. 244).
3. Cf. Schmoekel (1955, p. 8) and Goettner-Abendroth (1980), pp. 65–66.
4. Schmoekel (1955, p. 14).
5. Falkenstein (1939, pp. 96–97).
6. Ranke-Graves (1986, p. 13).
7. Goettner-Abendroth (1980); see also Schreier (1982).
8. Hofmannsthal (Reclam:n.d.).

Chapter 5   Zeus and Hera: Couples in Conflict
1. Willi (1982, pp. 110–11).
2. Cf. *Ibid.*, pp. 110ff.
3. Albee (1962, pp. 13–15).
4. Homer (1951).
5. Goettner-Abendroth (1980, p. 33).
6. Pauly (1979, vol. 2, pp. 1028ff).
7. Cf. Ranke-Graves (1986, p. 42) and Goettner-Abendroth (1980, pp. 41–45).
8. Cf. Ranke-Graves (1986, p. 42).

Chapter 6   Merlin and Viviane: The Wise Old Man and the Young Girl
1. Dorst (1981).
2. F. Hetmann in White (1980).

3. *Herder Symbol Dictionary* (1986).
4. Boron (1980, pp. 175–85).
5. F. Hetmann in White (1980, p. 237).
6. Goettner-Abendroth (1980).
7. Zimmer (1977).
8. Riedel (1983).
9. Zimmer (1977, p. 203).
10. *Herder Lexicon, Germanische und Keltische Mythologie* (1982).
11. Boron (1980, p. 194).
12. Goethe (1961, p. 262ff).
13. Goethe (1961, p. 262).
14. Goethe (1961, pp. 262–63).
15. *Ibid.*
16. *Ibid.*, p. 263.
17. Frisch (1975, pp. 71ff.).

Chapter 7 **Brother Husband and Sister Wife: Solidarity and Equipoise**
1. Cocteau (1929).
2. Vielhauer (1979, pp. 57–59).
3. Schmoekel (1956).
4. Binswanger (1962).

Chapter 8 **A Critical Appraisal: The Anima and Animus Concept of C. G. Jung**
1. von Franz (1986, p. 195).
2. Jung, "Letter of January 2, 1957," in *Letters* (1975, vol. 2).
3. Wilhelm and Jung (1962, p. 115).
4. Cf. Porkert (1979).
5. Jung (1966, vol. 7, par. 331).
6. Jung (1968, vol. 13, p. 118).
7. Jung (1968, vol. 9, part 1, par. 114).
8. Jung (1970, vol. 14, par. 646).
9. Jung, "Letter of November 12, 1957," in *Letters* (1975, vol. 2).
10. Jung (1966, vol. 7, par. 336).
11. Jung (1970, vol. 18, par. 589).
12. Jung (1968, vol. 13, par. 744).
13. Jung (1968, vol. 9, part 2, par. 33).
14. *Ibid.*, par. 40.
15. Jung (1970, vol. 14, par. 356).
16. Jung (1968, vol. 9, part 2, par. 34).
17. *Ibid.*, par. 53.
18. *Ibid.*, par. 33.
19. Wilhelm and Jung (1962, p. 116)
20. Jung (1966, vol. 7, par. 301).
21. Jung (1968, vol. 9, part 2, par. 24).
22. Jung (1968, vol. 9, part 1, par. 59).
23. Jung (1968, vol. 13, par. 673).
24. *Ibid.*, par. 224.
25. *Ibid.*
26. von Franz (1986, p. 195).
27. Jung (1970, vol. 14, par. 424).
28. *Ibid.*, par. 673.
29. Jung (1968, vol. 9, part 1, par. 393).
30. Gregory Bateson, cited in Capra (1983, p. 22).
31. Jung (1968, vol. 9, part 2, par. 28).
32. Jung (1970, vol. 14, par. 760).

33. Hillman (1985).
34. Jung (1970, vol. 14, pars. 222–23).
35. Neumann (1954, p. 42).
36. Jung (1970, vol. 14, par. 133).
37. Jung (1968, vol. 9, part 1, par. 490).
38. Jung (1968, vol. 14, par. 283).
39. Eccles and Popper (1977, p. 337–38).
40. Willi (1982).
41. Eccles and Popper (1977).
42. *Ibid.*
43. *Ibid.*, p. 334.

Bibliography

Albee, E. *Who's Afraid of Virginia Woolf?* New York: Atheneum, 1962.

Bachman, I. "Der Fall Franza" ["The Case of Franza"]. In *Gesammelte Werke*, vol. 3. C. Koschel, I. Weidenbaum, and C. Meunster, eds. Munich: Piper, 1978.

Binswanger, L. *Grundformen und Erkenntnis Menshlichen Daseins*. Zurich: M. Neihan, 1942.

Bloch, E. *Das Prinzip Hoffnung*. Frankfurt: Suhrkamp. 1959.

Boron, R. *Merlin—Der Kuender des Graals [Merlin—Messenger of the Grail]*. Stuttgart: 1980.

Capra, F. *Wendezeit [Turning Point]*. Munich: 1983.

Cocteau, J. *Les Enfants Terribles*. Paris: B. Grasset, 1929.

Dorst, T. *Merlin oder in das Wuste Land*. Frankfurt: Suhrkamp, 1981.

Eccles, J., and Popper, K. *The Self and Its Brain*. New York: Springer International, 1977.

Falkenstein, A. *Zeitschrift fuer Assyriologie und Verwandte Gebiete [Journal of Assyriology and Related Areas]*, vol. 11. 1939.

——————, and Soden, W. *Sumerische und Akkadische Hymnen und Gebete [Sumerian and Akkadian Hymns and Prayers]*. Zurich: Artemis-Verlag, 1953.

von Franz, M.-L. The Process of Individuation. In *Man and His Symbols*, C. G. Jung *et al.*, eds. Garden City, N.J.: 1968.

Frisch, M. *Montauk*. G. Skelton, ed. New York: Harcourt Brace Jovanovich, 1976.

——————. *Als der Krieg zu Ende ging [When the War Ended]*. In *Gesammelte Werke in Zeitlicher Folge*. Frankfurt: Suhrkamp, 1976.

Geissler, H. W. *Wovon du Traeumst [Whereof You Dream]*. Zurich: 1955.

Goethe, J. W. von. *Der West-östliche Divan*. H. Maltzahn, ed. Frankfurt: Suhrkamp-Taschenbuch-Verlag, 1961.

——————. *The West-eastern Divan*, J. Whaley, trans. Munich: 1979.

Goettner-Abendroth, H. *Die Goettin und ihr Heros [The Goddess and her Hero]*. Munich: Frauenoffensive, 1980.

Herder Lexikon, Germanische und Keltische Mythologie Freiburg i B: 1982.

Herder Symbol Dictionary. B. Matthews, trans. Wilmette, IL: Chiron Publications, 1986.

Hillman, J. *Anima: an Anatomy of a Personified Notion*. Dallas: Spring Publications, 1985.

Hofmannsthal, H. *Der Rosenkavalier, Komoedie fuer Musik*. Berlin: S. Fischer, 1911.

Hohler, A. *Wozu das Alles? [What's It All For?]* Zurich: 1980.

Homer. *The Iliad*. R. Lattimore, trans. Chicago: University of Chicago Press, 1951.

Jung, C. G. *Aion: Researches into the Phenomenology of the Self*. In *Collected Works*, vol. 9, part 2. Princeton: Princeton University Press, 1968.

_____. *The Archetypes and the Collective Unconscious*. In *Collected Works*, vol. 9, part 1. Princeton: Princeton University Press, 1968.

_____. *Letters*. vol. 2. G. Adler and A. Jaffe, eds, R. Hull, trans. Princeton: Princeton University Press, 1975.

_____. Commentary on "The Secret of the Golden Flower." In *Alchemical Studies*. In *Collected Works*, vol. 13. Princeton: Princeton University Press, 1967.

_____. *Mysterium Coniunctionis*. In *Collected Works*, vol. 14. Princeton: Princeton University Press, 1970.

_____. The Relations Between the Ego and the Unconscious. In *Two Essays on Analytical Psychology*. In *Collected Works*, vol. 7. Princeton: Princeton University Press, 1966.

_____. *The Symbolic Life*. In *Collected Works*, vol. 18. Princeton: Princeton University Press, 1970.

Kast, V. *Trauern: Phasen und Chancen des Psychischen Prozesses [Mourning: Phases and Chances of the Psychic Process]*. Stuttgart: Kreuz-Verlag, 1982.

Leisi, E. *Paar und Sprache [Couple and Language]*. Heidelberg: Quelle and Meyer, 1978.

Maupassant, G. de. Indiscretion. In *The Works of Guy de Maupassant*, vol. 6. A. McMaster *et al.,* trans. London and New York: Classic Publishing, 1911.

Neumann, E. *The Origins and History of Consciousness*. Princeton: Princeton University Press, 1954.

Ovid. *The Metamorphoses*, A. Watts, trans. San Francisco: North Point Press, 1980.

Pauly, A. *Der Kleine Pauly, Lexikon oer Antike [Lexicon of Antiquity]*. K. Ziegler, W. Sontheiner, and H. Gartner, eds. Stuttgart: A Druckenmuller, 1964–75, 1979.

Porkert, M. *The Theoretical Foundations of Chinese Medicine*. Cambridge, Mass.: M.I.T. Press, 1979.

Ranke-Graves, R. *Griechische Mythologie [Greek Mythology]*. Hamburg: Rowohlt Verlag, 1986.

Riedel, I. *Farben [Colors]*. Stuttgart: Kreuz-Verlag, 1983.

Schmoekel, Hartmut. *Das Land Sumer [The Land Sumer]*. Stuttgart: 1955.

_____. *Heilige Hochzeit und Hoheslied [Sacred Marriage and the Songs of Songs]*. Wiesbaden: F. Steiner, 1956.

Schreier, J. *Goettinnen [Goddesses]*. Munich: Frauenoffensive, 1982.

Vielhauer, I. *Bruder und Schwester: Untersuchungen und Betrachtungen zu einem Urmotive Zwischenmenschlicher Beziehung [Brother and Sister: Investigations and Observations of a Primordial Motif in Interpersonal Relationships]*. Bonn: Bouvier, 1979.

White, T. H. ed. *Das Buch Merlin*. F. Hetmann, ed. Cologne: Eugen Diederichs Verlag, 1980.

Wilhelm, R., and Jung, C. G. *The Secret of the Golden Flower*. New York: Harcourt, Brace and World, 1962.

Willi, J. *Couples in Collusion*. New York: Jason Aronson, 1982.

Zimmer, H. *Abenteuer und Fahrten der Seele: Vier Episoden aus den Sagen um die Goettin [Adventures and Journeys of the Soul: Four Episodes from Sagas about the Goddess]*. Cologne: 1977.

Index